The Greatest Travel Tips

KYOTO

Kyoto - The Capital of Old

Kyoto served as Japan's Imperial City for more than a thousand years - from the time Emperor Kammu relocated the capital there in 794 to the 19th century when Tokyo became the capital – and it is still home to many important cultural assets, including 17 World Heritage Sites. From wooden buildings made with traditional construction techniques to beautiful statutes of the Buddha and immaculately-kept gardens, it has much to offer to the many tourists who visit. It is surrounded by mountains to the north, east and west, and the pure waters of the Kamo-gawa flow right through the downtown core, providing people with a way to escape to nature at any time of year, whether for the cherry blossoms in spring, or for the incredible colors of autumn.

京 都 旅 行 案 内

～古都、京都～

794 年桓武天皇が都と定めて以来 1000 年余り、首都が東京に移るまで日本の王都であり続けました。今も17の世界遺産をはじめとした貴重な文化財が数多く残されています。伝統的工法の木造建築や美しい仏像、手入れの行き届いた庭園などは、多くの観光客を魅了しています。また、街を囲むように東・北・西に連なる山々や繁華街の中心を流れる鴨川の清流など自然も豊かで、春の桜や秋の紅葉など四季折々、魅力的な表情を楽しめます。

The Greatest Travel Tips KYOTO

京都旅行案内

Contents

Explanatory notes 凡例

☎ Telephone number 電話番号
🚶 Access 交通
🕐 Business hours 営業時間
🆑 Regular holiday 定休日
[¥] Fee 料金

Kyoto —A Quick Outline

京都 アウトラインガイド

Here is a little bit about Kyoto's seven most popular areas. 京都の主な7エリアの特徴を簡単に知っておこう。

Around Kinkaku-ji Temple ◎金閣寺周辺

Kinukake-no-michi is a 2.5 km sightseeing road that runs along the foot of Mount Kinugasa. Visitors to the area will find Kinkaku-ji Temple(→P14), Ryoan-ji Temple(→P22), and Ninna-ji Temple(→P17) World Cultural Heritage Sites and other temples nearby.

衣笠山の山麓の全長約2.5kmの観光道路・きぬかけの路沿いに、世界文化遺産の金閣寺（→ P14）、龍安寺（→ P22）、仁和寺（→ P17）などが点在。

Arashiyama ◎嵐山（→ P38）

This lush and scenic area of the city has the famed bridge over the Katsuragawa River called Togetsukyo, walking paths through the bamboo groves, and much more. It is also home to Buddhist and Shinto religious institutions such as Tenryu-ji Temple(→P20).

自然豊かな嵐山、桂川にかかる渡月橋、竹林の中の道など、風光明媚なエリア。天龍寺（→ P20）をはじめ多くの社寺がある。

Nijo-jo Castle & Kyoto Imperial Palace
◎二条城・京都御所

This area is the former heart of Kyoto's government and economy, and features the former castle of the Tokugawa Shogunate, Nijo-jo Castle(→P32), and the former home of the Emperor, Kyoto Imperial Palace(→P34).

かつて、京都の政治・経済の中心だったエリアで、徳川将軍の居城であった二条城（→ P32）や明治初期まで天皇が暮らした京都御所（→ P34）などが残る。

Map

Kinkaku-ji Temple(Rokuon-ji Temple)
Around Kinkaku-ji Temple
Ryoan-ji Temple
Ninna-ji Temple
Ryoan-ji Sta.

Arashiyama

JR Sanin Line (Sagano Line)

Tenryu-ji Temple
Keifuku Ry. Arashiyama Line

Togetsu-kyo
Hnakyu Arashiyama Sta.

Hankyu Ry. Arashiyama Line

Subway Tozai Line (Randen)

Katsura Imperial Villa

Katsura Sta.

Katsuragawa River

Hankyu Ry. Kyoto Line

JR Tokaido Line/JR Kyoto Line

JR Tokaido Shinkansen

To Nagaoka-kyo Sta.
To Yamazaki Sta.

To Shin Osaka Sta.

Around Kyoto Station ◎京都駅周辺

In the hub of Kyoto Tourism, visitors are only steps away from World Cultural Heritage Sites such as Nishi Hongan-ji Temple(→P9) and Toji Temple(→P27). Choose from a variety of souvenirs on sale in the station building.

京都観光の拠点。世界文化遺産の西本願寺（→ P9）、東寺（→ P27）は徒歩圏内。駅ビル内はみやげ店が多く入る。

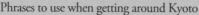

Phrases to use when getting around Kyoto

Unlike many Japanese cities, Kyoto city center is laid out in a grid pattern and each road is named. When traveling north towards the palace, people say they are "going up" or "agaru" and when heading south, they say they are "going down" or "sagaru." If going east, they say "higashi-iru," or "going into the east" and in the same way, they say "nishi-iru" when "going into the west."

◆京都の　京都市内中心部は碁盤の目のように縦横に規則正しく区画され、通りごとに名前が付いている。
歩き方の　京都御所近くの北に行くことを「上る」、そして逆の南へ行くことを「下る」、東や西へ行くこと
表現　　は「東入（い）る」「西入（い）る」という。

Around Ginkaku-ji Temple ◎銀閣寺周辺

A number of famous temples sit at the foot of Higashi-yama, including Ginkaku-ji Temple(→P15) and Nanzen-ji Temple(→P18), and the area around Heian Jingu Shrine(→P16) is the arts district and has a number of museums. Head over to the Lake Biwa Canal to the 2 km long path known as The Path of Philosophy, (Tetsugaku-no Michi).

東山の麓には銀閣寺（→ P15）や南禅寺（→ P18）などの有名寺院が多く、平安神宮（→ P16）周辺は美術館が集まるアートゾーン。琵琶湖疏水沿いに続く全長約 2km の散歩道・哲学の道がある。

Around Kiyomizu-dera Temple ◎ 清水寺周辺

The area around Kiyomizu-dera Temple(→P10) is full of famous temples and shrines, and the various approach roads are lined with souvenir shops and restaurants.

清水寺（→ P10）の門前町で、参道の二年坂、産寧坂、清水坂、茶わん坂にはみやげ店や食事処が集中し、有名な社寺も多い。

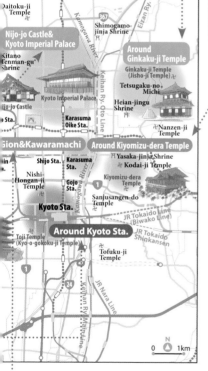

河 Kamigamo-jinja
Shinto Shrine

Subway
Karasuma Line

Daitoku-ji
Temple

367

Shimogamo-jinja
Shrine

Eizan Ry.

**Nijo-jo Castle&
Kyoto Imperial Palace**

Kitano
Tenman-gu
Shrine

**Around
Ginkaku-ji Temple**

Ginkaku-ji Temple
(Jisho-ji Temple)

Kyoto Imperial Palace

Tetsugaku-no
Michi

jo-jo Castle

Heian-jingu
Shrine

Karasuma
Oike Sta.

Nanzen-ji
Temple

Sta.

Gion&Kawaramachi

Around Kiyomizu-dera Temple

in.

Shijo Sta.

Karasuma
Sta.

Yasaka-jinja Shrine
Kodai-ji Temple

Nishi-
Hongan-ji
Temple

Gojo
Sta.

Kiyomizu-dera
Temple

Kyoto Sta.

Sanjusangen-do
Temple

JR Tokaido Line
(Biwako Line)

Around Kyoto Sta.

JR Tokaido
Shinkansen

Toji Temple
(Kyo-o-gokoku-ji Temple)

Tofuku-ji
Temple

24

JR Nara Line

N

0   1km

Gion & Kawaramachi ◎祇園・河原町

Kyoto's downtown area, where you will mainly find locals shopping and enjoying a meal. Gion is one of Kyoto's *kagai*, so with the maiko(→P50) and the older eating establishments found there, visitors get a taste of Kyoto flavor.

京都一の繁華街。地元の人々が主に買い物や食事をする場所。また、舞妓さん（→ P50）がいる花街・祇園は京都の風情満点で、老舗料理店などが軒を連ねる。

1 Fushimi Inari-Taisha Shrine

| 伏見稲荷大社 |

奉納

奥之仙
一奥之仙

The Thousand Torii : Known as the Thousand Torii, there are actually roughly 10 thousand torii at the shrine. The red color was meant to ward off evil.

千本鳥居：境内には約1万基の鳥居が。
朱色は魔除けを意味

The impressive tunnel of red *torii*

❁ 赤い鳥居のトンネルが圧巻

Fushimi Inari-Taisha Shrine is one of Kyoto's most popular spots among tourists from overseas. It is also the head shrine of more than 30,000 shrines around Japan dedicated to the worship of the god Inari. Inari has been worshipped since ancient times as god of business prosperity, and the shrine was founded in 711. The red gates are known as *torii* and they were considered the boundary between the world of gods and the world of humanity. The shrine is famous for its tunnel of *torii* each of which was donated by a shrine visitor hoping for divine intervention from Inari.

外国人に人気№1の観光スポット。全国各地に3万社ある稲荷神社の総本宮。711年創建、古くから商売繁盛の神様として信仰される。鳥居は神と人間の住む世界を分けるもの。この参道に立てられた多くの鳥居は、参詣者の願い事が成就したお礼として寄進されたもの。

☎075-641-7331 📍P71-C5
🚶 Near JR Inari Station
🈁🕐ⓘ Open to the public

Sttopping alone the way 立ち寄りスポット

Sohonke Inari-ya
総本家いなりや

Pick up a pack of senbei rice crackers shaped like fox heads. From 370yen (3 per package).
キツネの顔をかたどった名物のきつね煎餅 370円～（3枚入）。

☎075-641-1166 📍P71-C4
🚶 3 minute walk from JR Inari Station
🕗 8:30-17:30 🈲 Friday

1. Ema : Shrine visitors write their prayers on plaques called ema. Many ema are painted with pictures of the heads of foxes, one of the symbols of Inari. *2. Omokaru-ishi :* The mysterious stone is said to grant wishes. *3. Yotsu-tsuji :* A famous intersection on the walkway that provides a great view of the city of Kyoto. *4. Kitsune :* The foxes that are said to be the attendants of the god Inari.

1. 絵馬：キツネの顔の絵馬がたくさん奉納されている *2.* おもかる石：願い事が叶うか占ってみよう *3.* 四ツ辻：分岐点、京都市街の景色が見られる *4.* キツネ：稲荷大神の使いとされるキツネの像

Inafuku
稲福

Inari sushi. From 130 yen a piece. A popular snack to pick up at Fushimi Inari-Taisha Shrine.

いな寿司1個130円〜は伏見稲荷大社の名物メニュー。

☎ 075-641-1138 　♥P71-C4
🚶 3 minute walk from JR Inari Station 🕐 9:00-17:00 🔒 2nd, 3rd, 4th Tuesday every month

Nezame-ya
祢ざめ家

Established in 1540. Grilled quail served with a secret sauce. 800 yen per skewer.

1540年創業。秘伝ダレを使ったうずらの焼鳥は1串800円。

☎ 075-641-0802 　♥P71-C4
🚶 2 minute walk from JR Inari Station 🕐 10:00-18:00 (Last orders 17:30) 🔒 Unscheduled

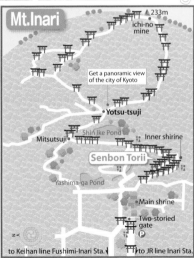

O-yama-meguri : The mountain pilgrimage route from the Inner shrine to the peak of Mt. Inari. The four km round trip to Ichi-no-mine and back takes about two hours. Shrines to a number of gods can be found along the route.

お山巡り：奥社から稲荷山山頂・一の峰まで往復4km、約2時間の巡拝コース。道中には数多の祠が祀られている。

World Cultural Heritage Sites

| 世界文化遺産 |

The 17 treasures of Kyoto

✿ 京都の 17 の宝

In 1994, 16 temples and shrines and one castle were collectively designated a UNESCO World Cultural Heritage Site called Historic Monuments of Ancient Kyoto. They are all world-class tourist spots.

1994年、京都の16寺社と1城がユネスコの世界文化遺産「古都京都の文化財」に登録された。いずれも世界の観光スポットだ。

Okuhiei Driveway
Arashiyama Takao Parkway
JR Sagano Line
JR Kosei Line
Lake Biwa
Kyoto
Tokaido-Shinkansen
Meishin Highway
JR Kyoto Line
To Nagoya
Uji
JR Nara Line
To Shin-Osaka

*Enryaku-ji Temple grounds are located on the border between Otsu City, Shiga Prefecture and Sakyo Ward, Kyoto.
※延暦寺は滋賀県大津市から京都市左京区にわたる

1 Kamigamo-jinja Shinto Shrine (☞P31)

上賀茂神社

This is one of the oldest Shrines in Kyoto. Both this Shrine and Shimogamo-jinja Shrine are famous for the Aoi-matsuri Festival (→ 98) held on May 15 every year.
京都最古の神社の一つ。毎年5/15の葵祭(→p98)で下鴨神社とともに有名。

2 Shimogamo-jinja Shrine

下鴨神社 (☞P31)

Surrounding the approach to the shrine is an old-growth forest called Tadasu-no-mori. Along with Kamigamo-jinja Shinto Shrine, this is one of the oldest shrines in Kyoto.
原生林「糺の森」が参道を包む。上賀茂神社と並ぶ古社。

3 Toji Temple (Kyo-o-gokoku-ji Temple) (☞P27)

東寺(教王護国寺)

This temple is famous for having the tallest wooden five-story pagoda (about 55m) in Japan and a three-dimensional mandala that relates the esoteric teachings of Shingon Buddhism.
日本一の高さ(約55m)の木造の五重塔や真言密教の教えを仏像群で表現した立体曼荼羅が有名。

4 Kiyomizu-dera Temple

清水寺 (☞P10)

The main hall has the famous Kiyomizu-no-butai (Kiyomizu stage), which rests above a cliff and commands a panoramic view of Kyoto City.
崖に建つ本堂には有名な「清水の舞台」があり、京都市内を一望できる。

5 Enryaku-ji Temple 延暦寺

Headquarters of the Tendai sect, this temple was established in 788 by the Buddhist monk, Saicho, and many patriarchs of Japanese Buddhism trained here.
788年に最澄が開いた天台宗の総本山で、多くの日本仏教の各宗祖が修行した場所。

☎077-578-0001 ♀P70-D2
🚶 Near the Keihan Bus / Kyoto Bus Enryaku-ji Bus Center bus stop
¥ 700yen ⏱ 8:30-16:30
📅 Open year round 7 days a week

6 Daigo-ji Temple 醍醐寺

This temple is known for having the oldest wooden building in Kyoto Prefecture (a five-story pagoda completed in 951), as well as a collection of roughly 150,000 temple treasures.

京都府内最古の木造建築物・五重塔（951年完成）や15万点にも及ぶ寺宝があることで知られる。

☎075-571-0002 ♥P71-D5 🚶12 minute walk from Daigo Station on the Tozai subway line｜¥｜600yen each to enter Sanbo-in, the Reiho-kan museum, Garan (Kondo Hall and five-story pagoda) and Kami-daigo ⏰ 9:00 – 17:00 (Until 16:00 from the Mon. following the 1st Sun. in Dec. to the end of Feb.. Admission up to 30 minutes before closing time) 📅Open year round 7 days a week (except for the Reiho-kan museum)

7 Ninna-ji Temple 仁和寺 (☞P17)

This temple was rebuilt after being burned down in the Onin War (1467) and on other occasions. It is famous for its late-blooming Omuro-zakura cherry blossom trees.

応仁の乱（1467年）などの焼失から再興。遅咲きの御室桜で知られる。

8 Byodo-in Temple 平等院

Established in 1052, this temple was build as a reprsentation the Pure Land world of Amida Buddha. The Hoo-do (Phoenix Hall) appears on the Japanese 10-yen coin.

1052年創建。仏教の極楽浄土の世界を表現した寺院。日本の10円硬貨にデザイン。

☎0774-21-2861 ♥P71-D6 🚶10 minute walk from Uji Station on the JR line｜¥｜600yen (Additional 300yen to enter the Phoenix Hall) ⏰ 8:30-17:30 (9:00-17:00 for the Hoshokan museum) 📅Open year round 7 days a week

9 Ujikami-jinja Shrine 宇治上神社

Constructed some time in or around the 11th century, the Honden Hall is the oldest extant shrine building in Japan.

本殿は11世紀頃に建てられ、現存する神社建築としては日本最古のもの。

☎0774-21-4634 ♥P71-D6 🚶5 minute walk from the JR Bus Togano-o bus stop ｜¥｜Free ⏰ 9:00-16:30 📅Open year round 7 days a week

10 Kosan-ji Temple 高山寺

This temple houses the Choju-jinbutsu-giga (Scrolls of Frolicking Animals and Humans), scrolls with depictions of personified animals that is said to be the origin of Japanese manga.

日本の漫画のはじまりとされる、動物を擬人化した絵巻「鳥獣人物戯画」を所蔵。

☎075-861-4204 ♥P70-A2 🚶5 minute walk from the JR Bus Togano-o bus stop ｜¥｜800yen ⏰ 8:30-17:00 📅Open year round 7 days a week

11 Saiho-ji Temple (Koke-dera Temple) 西芳寺（苔寺）

Also called Koke-dera (moss temple), this temple is famous for the garden entirely covered by approximately 120 kinds of moss.

約120種の苔で一面を覆い尽くされた庭園が有名で「苔寺」とも呼ばれる。

☎075-391-3631 (reservation required) ♥P71-A4 🚶Near the Koke-dera Suzumushi-dera bus stop ｜¥｜From 3,000yen (includes service fees) ⏰ To visit, application must be made by sending a return postcard no later than one week in advance 📅Open year round 7 days a week

12 Tenryu-ji Temple 天龍寺 (☞P20)

You shouldn't miss the Sogen-chi Garden (Sogen Pond Garden), a strolling garden that covers an immense area of about 4,000m² and incorporates, or "borrows," the scenery of Arashiyama.

広さ約4000㎡に及ぶ、嵐山を借景とした池泉回遊式の曹源池庭園は必見。

13 Kinkaku-ji Temple (Rokuon-ji Temple) (☞P14) 金閣寺（鹿苑寺）

This temple used to be the villa of Shogun Ashikaga Yoshimitsu. A beautiful harmony exists between the shining gold of the Kinkaku pavilion and the garden.

将軍・足利義満の元別荘。金色に輝く楼閣「金閣」と庭園の調和が美しい寺。

14 Ginkaku-ji Temple (Jisho-ji Temple) 銀閣寺（慈照寺）(☞P15)

This temple was built by Shogun Ashikaga Yoshimasa. His sense of beauty and the Zen spirit of wabi-sabi (simplicity and quietude) are apparent everywhere.

将軍・足利義政が建立。義政の美意識・禅の精神「わびさび」が随所に投影されている。

15 Ryoan-ji Temple 龍安寺 (☞P22)

The karesansui rock garden comprised only of 15 rocks and white sand is known worldwide and has even been praised by Queen Elizabeth II.

15の石と白砂だけで構成された枯山水の石庭は世界的に有名で、エリザベス女王も称賛した。

16 Nishi Hongan-ji Temple 西本願寺

This is the head temple of the Jodo Shinshu sect. You can still see splendid architecture from the Momoyama period, including the Karamon Gate.

浄土真宗本願寺派の本山。唐門など桃山文化の壮麗な建築が残る。

☎075-371-5181 ♥P72-B2 🚶Near the Kyoto City Bus Nishi Honganji-mae bus stop ｜¥｜Free ⏰ 5:30-17:00 (Until 17:30 in Mar., Apr., Sep. and Oct. Until 18:00 from May to Aug.) 📅Open year round 7 days a week

17 Nijo-jo Castle 二条城 (☞P32)

This is one of the castles built by the Tokugawa Shogunate. Must-see parts include the wall paintings in the Ninomaru Palace painted by Kano school artists and the gorgeous ceilings.

徳川将軍の居城の一つ。二の丸御殿の狩野派の障壁画や天井の豪華な装飾がみどころ。

3 *Kiyomizu-dera Temple*

| 清水寺 |

The most popular temple in Kyoto

✿ 京都No.1の人気寺院

Every year, more than five million people visit Kiyomizu-dera, a temple located on Mt. Otowa that was founded as a hermitage by a Buddhist priest named Enchin in 778. Enshrined here is the Kiyomizu-gata eleven-headed, thousand-armed bodhisattva Kannon, who is only revealed to the public once every 33 years. There are 30 buildings on the temple grounds, which are an expansive 130,000 meters squared. Visitors can see historical pagodas, belfries, and spots such as the famed Kiyomizu-no-butai.

年間 500 万人以上が訪れる。778 年、夢でお告げを受けた延鎮上人が音羽山に草庵を建てたのが始まり。本尊は 33 年に一度しか公開されない秘仏の清水型十一面千手観音。13 万㎡もの広大な敷地には「清水の舞台」をはじめ塔や鐘楼など約 30 の堂塔が点在しみどころが多い。

At certain times during spring, summer and autumn, the temple is illuminated and takes on a truly magical atmosphere.
春・夏・秋には期間限定でライトアップされ、境内は幻想的な雰囲気になる

☎075-551-1234 ♥P80-C4
🚶10 minute walk from the Kyoto City Bus Gojo-zaka or Kiyomizu-michi bus stop
¥400yen ⏱6:00 – 18:00 (Subject to change according to the season) ㋐Open year round 7 days a week

10

Nio-mon (Deva gate)
仁王門

The magnificent main gate is 14m tall and 10m wide, and is known as Akamon or Red Gate due to its beautiful color. The gate is flanked by 3.65m tall statues of the Nio, the Buddha's two guardians, who protect the temple.

棟高約 14 m、幅 10 m もの大きな正門は、赤色が美しいことから「赤門」と呼ばれる。門の両脇には高さ 3.65 m もの仁王像が寺を警護する。

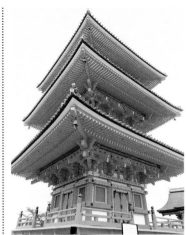

Sanju-no-to
(Three-story pagoda)
三重塔

This beautiful red pagoda was built in 1632 and is 31m high. The inside is not open to the general public. It features richly colored esoteric Buddhist paintings as well as celestial maidens and dragons painted on the ceilings and pillars.

朱色が美しい 1632 年に建てられた高さ 31m の塔で、内部は非公開。天井・柱などには密教仏画や飛天・龍が極彩色で描かれている。

Otowa-no-taki
(Otowa waterfall)
音羽の滝

This waterfall is fed by a single source that is split into three streams, and each falling stream is said to grant a different form of wish. The streams symbolize academics, love, and longevity. Drink from them to make your wishes come true.

滝の水は三筋に別れて流れ落ちる。「学問」「恋愛」「延命」の水とされ、飲んだ水の願いが叶うといわれる。

Kiyomizu-no-butai (Kiyomizu stage)
清水の舞台

The Kiyomizu stage is the large deck that juts out from the main hall. It was built upon a cliff, stands about 12m tall, and is supported by an incredible lattice-like assembly of timber joined together without a single nail.

舞台とは本堂からせり出した部分のこと。高さ 12 m の舞台は切り立った崖に建ち、釘を一本も使わずに木材を格子状に見事に組み上げている。

Around Kiyomizu-dera Temple

| 清水寺周辺 |

Sloping streets where you can enjoy shopping and eating

✿ 買い物とグルメが楽しい坂道

Kiyomizu-dera Temple is surrounded by sloping streets. Ninen-zaka, Sannei-zaka, Kiyomizu-zaka, and Chawan-zaka are all lined with souvenir shops and restaurants. This makes the area popular among people looking to visit the temple, while getting in some shopping and having a bite to eat at the same time. The area has been designated a Preservation District for Groups of Traditional Buildings, and it retains traces of the ancient capital and provides you with many photo opportunities.

清水寺周辺は二年坂、産寧坂、清水坂、茶わん坂の坂道が集まる。各道の両側にはみやげ店や飲食店が立ち並び、寺社巡りと買い物とグルメを一緒に楽しめる一大観光スポットだ。また界隈は伝統的建造物群保存地区で古都の町並みが残り記念撮影ポイントも多い。

Kodai-ji Temple
高台寺

Maruyama-park
←円山公園

Kodaiji Rakusho
(warabi-mochi and other sweets)
高台寺 洛匠

Ten-qoo-ann
天空庵

Ishibe-koji Alley
石塀小路

❶

Nene-no-michi Path
ねねの道

This cobblestone lane was named after Toyotomi Hideyoshi's wife, Nene, who established Kodai-ji Temple.
高台寺を創建した豊臣秀吉の妻「ねね」の名が付いた石畳の道。

Photo spots

Ishibe-koji Alley is a quiet lane lined with stone walls and you'll find traditional Japanese inns and restaurants.
石塀小路は石塀が続く静かな路地で、老舗旅館や料亭が立ち並ぶ

Higashi-oji Street
東大路通

Bus stops:
Higashiyama Yasui
東山安井

❶ Ten-qoo-ann
天空庵

This shop sells Japanese variety goods and craftwork jewelry procured from all over Japan. Glass bead *tombo-dama* pierced earings: 900yen.
日本の全国各地から仕入れた和雑貨や工芸品のアクセサリーなどを販売。トンボ玉のピアス 900 円。

☎075-531-3111 ♥P80-B3
🚶5 minute walk from the Kyoto City Bus Higashiyama Yasui bus stop
🕚11:00 – 18:00
Tuesdays

❷ Minatoya
港屋

This shop specializes in items related to Takehisa Yumeji (1884-1934), a painter whose body of work included many *bijinga* (pictures of beautiful women).
多くの美人画を残した画家・竹久夢二（1884-1934）のグッズ専門店。

☎075-551-5552 ♥P80-C4
🚶5 minute walk from the Kyoto City Bus Kiyomizu-michi bus stop 🕙10:00 – 18:00
Open year round 7 days a week

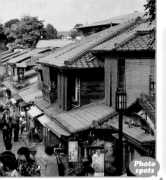

Photo spots

You can get an excellent photo of the sprawling city from the top of Ninen-zaka's gentle slope.
二年坂は緩やかな坂道。上の方から町並みの風景も入れて撮影しよう

Kiyomizu-dera Temple
清水寺

❸ Shoeido 松栄堂

Popular products at this 300 year old incense specialty shop include authentic incense sets and sachets.
Stick incense: 864yen.

300年続くお香の専門店。本格的なお香セットや匂い袋も人気だ。スティック型お香864円。

☎075-532-5590 📍P80-C4
🚶10 minute walk from the Kyoto City Bus Kiyomizu-michi bus stop ⏰9:00 – 18:00
📅Open year round 7 days a week

Shoeido 松栄堂

❸

Kiyomizu-zaka Street 清水坂

Chawan-zaka (tea-bowl slope)Street 茶わん坂

❷ Minatoya 港屋

Sohonke Yudofu, Okutan 総本家ゆどうふ奥丹

❹

Shichimiya Honpo 七味家本舗

Ninen-zaka Street 二年坂

Centrally located among the temples and shrines in the vicinity, this street has many gift shops that cater to worshippers.
周辺の寺社を中心に発展したため参拝客向けのみやげ物店が多い。

Sannei-zaka Street 産寧坂

This slope is 100 meters long, lined with traditional wooden buildings, and has stone steps along the way.
石の階段を含む100mの坂道で両側には伝統的な木造建築が立ち並ぶ。

This street was named for the "chawan" (tea bowl) and other Kiyomizuyaki pottery that is sold by many of the shops here.
茶碗などの清水焼を扱う店が道沿いに軒を連ねることが名の由来。

Yasaka Pagoda (Hokan-ji Temple) 八坂の塔 (法観寺)

Yasaka-dori Street 八坂通

Kongo-ji Temple (Yasaka-Koshin-do Temple) 金剛寺 (八坂庚申堂)

Bus stops: Kiyomizu-michi 清水道

Photo spots

Gojo-zaka Street 五条坂

❹ Shichimiya Honpo 七味家本舗

Founded 360 years ago, this shop sells shichimi and sansho, spices made from domestically grown chili peppers. Shichimi togarashi in bamboo container 702 yen.

創業360年、国産唐辛子を使った七味や山椒を扱う老舗。竹筒七味唐辛子702円。

☎075-551-0738 📍P80-C4
🚶10 minute walk from the Kyoto City Bus Kiyomizu-michi bus stop ⏰9:00 – 18:00 (Subject to change depending on the season)
📅Open year round 7 days a week

Bus stops: Gojo-zaka 五条坂

Gojo-dori Street 五条通

Yasaka-dori Street leads to the five-story Yasaka Pagoda, an excellent spot to take a photo.
八坂通は八坂の塔へ続く道。五重塔と一緒に写真を撮ろう

Around Kiyomizu-dera Temple ◉ 清水寺周辺

13

Kinkaku-ji Temple and Ginkaku-ji Temple

5

| 金閣寺と銀閣寺 |

1 Inside the third floor of the *shariden:* This golden room houses some of the Buddha's ashes.

2 *Rikushu-no Matsu* (**Land Boat Pine**)*:* The outspread branches of this beautiful pine tree look like a sailboat. The tree is about 600 years old.

3 *Houou:* Shining atop the roof of the pavilion is the legendary Chinese phoenix bird, a symbol of eternal life and power.

1 舎利殿の3層目内部：黄金の部屋。釈迦の遺骨「仏舎利」が安置される
2 陸舟の松：広げた枝が帆船の形になっている見事な松。樹齢約600年
3 鳳凰：屋根に輝く中国の伝説の鳥・鳳凰。永遠の命と権力を象徴する

Shariden(kinkaku, or Gold Pavilion): This building was destroyed by arson in 1950, but was rebuilt five years later. The interior is not open to the public.
舎利殿（金閣）：1950年に放火によって焼失したが、5年後に現在のものへ復元された。内部は非公開

○ *Kinkaku-ji Temple (Rokuon-ji Temple* 鹿苑寺)
☎075-461-0013 ♥P78-C1
🚶3 minute walk from the Kyoto City Bus Kinkakuji-michi bus stop
¥400yen
🕘9:00-17:00
🗓Open year round 7 days a week

Ashikaga Yoshimitsu
足利義満（1358〜1408）

Yoshimitsu rekindled trade with Ming Dynasty China and largely contributed to Japan's cultural development. In accordance with his wishes, Kinkaku was converted into a Zen temple after his death.
義満は、中国・明との貿易を盛んにして文化の発展に大きく貢献した。義満の死後、遺言により金閣は禅寺となった。

The "Gold" and "Silver" World Heritage sites

✿ 世界遺産の金と銀

Kinkaku-ji Temple was originally built in 1397 by Ashikaga Yoshimitsu, the third Muromachi shogun, as both a villa and a symbol of his power. The three-story Kinkaku (Golden Pavilion) now functions as a reliquary hall and is covered in approximately 20 kg of gold foil. Ginkaku-ji Temple was built in 1482 by Ashikaga Yoshimasa, the eighth Muromachi shogun. While the structure is based on the Kinkaku built by his grandfather, the Ginkaku (Silver Pavilion) is not actually covered in silver foil. In contrast to the Kinkaku, it has a serene and unadorned simplicity.

金閣寺は1397年、室町幕府3代将軍・足利義満が自身の権力の象徴として造営した山荘が始まり。三層の楼閣・舎利殿は約20kgもの金箔で覆われている。銀閣寺は1482年、室町幕府8代将軍・足利義政が造営。楼閣の基本的な構造は、祖父の義満が造った金閣をモデルとした。銀箔で覆われているわけではなく、金閣とは対照的に、簡素で落ち着いた外観だ。

Ashikaga Yoshimasa
足利義政（1436～1490）

Yoshimasa preferred art to politics and power struggles. His sophisticated taste is apparent in every aspect of Ginkaku-ji Temple, but he didn't live to see its completion.

義政は、政治や権力争いよりも芸術に親しんだ。その秀でたセンスが銀閣寺の随所にうかがえるが、完成を待たずしてこの世を去った。

Kannon-den Hall (Ginkaku, or Silver Pavilion): Enshrined within is a seated statue of the boddisattva Kannon. Near the hall is the Ginshadan, a layout of sand representing rippling waves of water, and a conical mound of white sand called Kogetsudai.
観音殿（銀閣）：観音菩薩坐像を安置。横には波紋を表現した銀沙灘と円錐台形の向月台と呼ばれる白砂の砂盛りが広がる。

④ **Togu-do Hall:** Both this hall and Ginkaku are National Treasures. Togu-do contains the Dojinsai, a room that was used by Yoshimasa as a study. Togu-do is shown to the public twice a year–in spring and autumn.
⑤ **Main hall door paintings :** These were painted by the great Edo-period painters Yosa Buson and Ike-no Taiga. They are shown to the public twice a year–in spring and autumn.
④ 東求堂：銀閣とともに国宝。義政の書斎だった"同仁斎"がある。年2回春秋公開あり
⑤ 本堂襖絵：江戸時代の名絵師・与謝蕪村、池大雅の作。年2回春秋公開あり

Ginkaku-ji Temple ○
(Jisho-ji Temple 慈照寺）
☎075-771-5725 📍P70-D3
🚶10 minute walk from the Kyoto City Bus Ginkakuji-michi bus stop, or 5-minute walk from the Kyoto City Bus Ginkakuji-mae bus stop
⌚8:30-17:00 (9:00-16:30 from Dec. to Feb)
㉚Open year round 7 days a week
¥500yen

6 The Cherry Blossoms of Kyoto | 京都の桜 |

Cascade of cherry blossoms from
a Yae-benishidarezakura (Plena Rosea cherry blossom tree)
シャワーのように降り注ぐヤエベニシダレザクラ

Heian-jingu Shrine
平安神宮

The spacious layout of this shrine features elegant pavilions reminiscent of former palace architecture, and four Shin-en, or "sacred gardens." There are about 300 sakura trees of 20 varieties located around the premises, their delicate blossoms reflected in the red-colored lacquer of the buildings. A stroll through the sakura trees takes about 30 minutes

広大な敷地内に、昔の宮殿建築を偲ばせる優雅な社殿を中心に、4つの神苑（日本庭園）を有する神社。約20種300本もの桜が境内を彩り、朱塗りの社殿にピンク色の桜が映える。約30分の桜散策が楽しめる。

Illuminated at night in early April.
4月上旬にはライトアップされる

☎075-761-0221 ♥P75-F1
🚶10 minute walk from Higashiyama Station on the Tozai subway line.
[¥] Free (600yen for the Shin-en gardens) ⏰6:00 – 18:00 (8:30 – 17:30 for Shin-en) *Subject to change according to the season 🗓Open year round 7 days a week

Japan's national flower coloring the ancient capital

✿ 古都を彩る日本の国花

The Japanese people have since ancient times loved the sakura(cherry blossom tree), cherishing it for the beauty of its blossoms and creating occasions to appreciate them at cherry-blossom viewing parties, or *hanami* (literally meaning "flower viewing"). Many shrines and temples in Kyoto are famous for their cherry blossoms, among which the Somei-yoshino and Beni-shidarezakura (Pendula Rosea) are just some of the large variety of sakura.

Some trees bloom early while others bloom late, allowing you to enjoy the cherry blossoms for about one month. As one might expect, Kyoto is very crowded when the cherry blossoms are in bloom.

古くからその姿を愛で、時には「花見」を開催し、日本人が愛してきた桜。京都の神社や寺院には桜の名所が多く、ソメイヨシノ、ベニシダレザクラなど種類も多い。早咲きから遅咲きのものまで約1か月間楽しめる。開花時期の京都は混雑必至だ。

Sakura season 桜の開花時期
Late March to Mid-April 3月下旬～4月中旬

This shrine has long been famous for viewing the cherry blossoms at night, the nighttime illumination also accentuating their beauty.
昔から夜桜の名所として知られ、ライトアップも美しい

Hirano-jinja Shrine
平野神社

The grounds of this shrine contain as many as 400 sakura of about 60 varieties, creating a long cherry viewing season of about a month and a half, during which you can see the popular Somei-yoshino variety in addition to more rare species.

境内には約60種400本もの桜が植わり、約1か月半という長期間に渡って定番のソメイヨシノから珍種まで多様な桜の見頃が続く。

☎075-461-4450 ♀P78-C2
🚶3 minute walk from the Kyoto City Bus Kinugasa-ko-mae bus stop [¥] Free ⏰6:00 – 17:00 (Omamori, "personal amulets," are sold from 9:00 Until 21:00 during cherry-blossom season)
🈺Open year round 7 days a week

Maruyama Park 円山公園

Opened in 1886, this is the oldest park in Kyoto City. In addition to the iconic weeping sakura, about 680 sakura have been planted throughout the park. Food and other stands open during cherry-blossom viewing season when the park bustles with visitors every day. The trees illuminated by lanterns at night are certainly a spectacle worth seeing.

☎075-561-1350 (Kyoto City Greenery Association) ♀P80-C2
🚶3 minute walk from the Kyoto City Bus Gion bus stop
[¥] ⏰ 🈺Park open to the public

1886年開園の京都市最古の公園。シンボルのシダレザクラをはじめ、約680本の桜が植えられている。シーズン中は露店が並び連日花見客で賑わう人気のスポット。提灯に照らされる夜桜も必見。

The weeping cherry tree located at the center of the park is about 90 years old.
園内中央のシダレザクラは樹齢約90年

Ninna-ji Temple 仁和寺

Founded in 888, the approximately 200 Omurozakura at this temple are known for being the latest blooming blossoms in Kyoto. The trees are low in height and bloom from the base, so you can enjoy viewing the delicately-tinted flowers from up close.

888年創建。京都一遅咲きで知られ、淡く色付く約200本の御室桜は背が低く根元から花が付くので、間近で桜を愛でることができる。

☎075-461-1155
♀P78-A2
🚶Near the Kyoto City Bus Omuro-Ninna-ji bus stop
[¥] 500yen ⏰9:00 – last admission 16:30 (16:00 from Dec. to Feb.)
🈺Open year round 7 days a week

The Omuro-zakura blooms as if delicately enshrouding the five-story pagoda in its blossoms.
五重塔を覆うように御室桜が咲き乱れる

17

Autumn Foliage in Kyoto

| 京都の紅葉 |

There are magnificent maple trees with large foliage on the both sides of the temple gate.
山門の両側には大きな枝葉の立派なカエデがある

Old temples shrouded in a colorful brocade of autumn leaves

✿ 錦に染まる秋の古寺

Along with spring, autumn is a popular sightseeing season in Kyoto, when people come to see the changing colors. Surrounded by mountains on three sides, Kyoto's rich natural landscape is the backdrop for the many maple trees planted on temple grounds when the leaves turn a crimson red with the arrival of autumn. There are many places famous for their autumn leaves in the area around Tetsugaku-no Michi (Path of Philosophy), and it is possible to stroll and visit them on foot.

紅葉の時期は、春に並ぶ京都の人気シーズン。三方を山に囲まれ、自然豊かな京都の寺社には多くのカエデが植えられ、秋の訪れとともに真紅に染まる。哲学の道周辺には、紅葉の名所が集まり、徒歩で巡ることができる。

Maple viewing season 紅葉時期
Mid-November to Mid-December 11月中旬〜12月中旬

Konkai Komyo-ji Temple 金戒光明寺

Both this temple and the adjacent Shinnyo-do Temple are famous for their autumn leaves. Particularly worth seeing are the areas around the temple gate and three-story pagoda, as well as the "Shiun-no-niwa" garden at the Ohojo building (open to the public for about one month during maple-viewing season). The leaves turn a breathtaking red when lit by the rays of the setting sun.

隣接する真如堂とともに紅葉の名所。特に山門や三重塔付近、大方丈「紫雲の庭」（紅葉時期の約1か月公開）は見事だ。夕日に照らされた紅葉がさらに赤く染まる様は格別。

☎075-771-2204 ♥P70-D3
🚶10 minute walk from the Kyoto City Bus Okazaki-michi bus stop ¥ Free (During maple-viewing season 800yen to enter the temple gate interior, 600yen to enter the Ohojo and Shiun-no Niwa, or 1,200yen for all two of them)
🕘9:00 – 16:00 Open year round 7 days a week

Heian-jingu Shrine
平安神宮

Nanzen-ji Temple
南禅寺

This is one of Kyoto's most famous *Zen* Buddhist temples. Climbing to the top of the 22m-high main gate (Sanmon) gives you a commanding view of the autumn leaves on the large temple grounds and of the Kyoto cityscape. There are also beautifully colored trees in the Hojo Teien, a karesansui garden consisting of white sand and large rocks.

京都を代表する禅寺。高さ22mの三門は有料で登ることができ、広い境内の紅葉と京都の町並みを見渡すことができる。方丈庭園の白砂と巨石からなる枯山水庭園の紅葉も美しい。

The design of the Suirokaku (Aqueduct) was based on the aqueducts of ancient Rome
古代ローマの水道橋を模した水路閣

The most vividly colored leaves are in the vicinity of the Sanmon gate
三門の周辺の紅葉が一番鮮やかだ

☎075-771-0365 ♥P70-D3
🚶10 minute walk from Keage Station on the Tozai subway line
¥ 500yen for the Hojo Teien, 500yen for the Sanmon 🕘Outer temple grounds always open to the public; Hojo Teien and Sanmon: 8:40 – 17:00 (16:30 from Dec. to Feb.)
Dec. 28 ~ 31

Honen-in Temple
法然院

This quiet old temple associated with the High Priest Honen, who founded the Jodo-shu Sect of Buddhism, is famous for its camellia and maple trees. Autumn leaves add a striking tinge of color to the quaintly simple thatched-roof temple gate.
The gates open early, giving you a special chance to visit first thing in the morning.

浄土宗の開祖・法然上人ゆかりの閑静な古寺で、椿と紅葉の名所として知られる。簡素な趣の萱葺きの山門を彩る紅葉が印象的。開門時間が早いので、早朝に訪れるのがおすすめ。

☎075-771-2420 ♀P70-D3
🚶5 minute walk from the Kyoto City Bus Minamida-cho bus stop 〔¥〕Free (500yen in spring and 800yen in autumn for special viewing) ⏰6:00 – 16:00 📅Open year round 7 days a week

20minute walk
徒歩 20 分

Ginkaku-ji Temple
銀閣寺
卍

Shinnyo-do Temple
真如堂
卍

Shirakawa-dori Street
白川通

N

20minute walk
徒歩 20 分

Shishigadani-dori Street
鹿ヶ谷通

Marutamachi-dori Street
丸太町通
卍

Eikan-do Temple
(Zenrin-ji Temple) 永観堂 （禅林寺）

This temple is known as "maple leaf Eikan-do" because the expansive premises are blanketed in luxuriant autumn foliage from approximately 3,000 maple trees. There is a particularly superb view from the hilltop on which the Taho-to pagoda is situated, and the statue of the temple's principle deity is famous as a rare depiction of Amida Nyorai glancing back.

約 3000 本もの紅葉が広い境内を包むように埋めつくす様から、「もみじの永観堂」といわれ、高台に立つ多宝塔から見渡す眺めは特に美しい。本尊の振り返った姿の阿弥陀如来像は有名。

☎075-761-0007 ♀P70-D3
🚶3 minute walk from the Kyoto City Bus Nanzen-ji Eikando-michi bus stop 〔¥〕600yen (1,000yen during Autumnal Exhibition) ⏰9:00 – last admission 16:00 📅Open year round 7 days a week

One temple highlight is the maple trees reflected upside down in the pond.
池の水面に映り込む
逆さ紅葉もみどころ

10minute walk
徒歩 10 分
卍

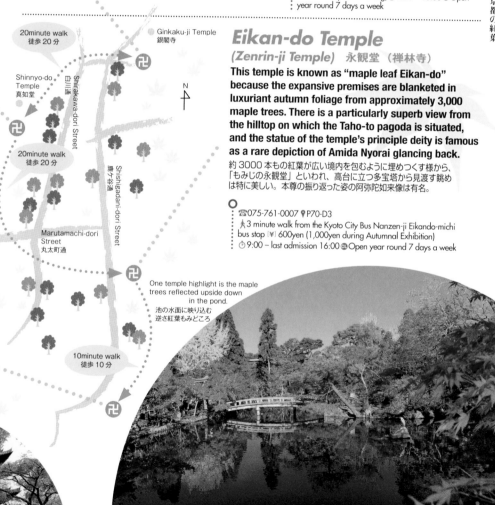

⑧ Japanese Gardens

| 日本庭園 |

Purify your soul
🍂 心洗われる空間

Kyoto is home to a variety of gardens built as far back as the Heian period (794-1185), and the different philosophies and values of each era can be seen in the style of each. Some better known types include chisen-teien, gardens built around a pond, karesansui-teien, gardens built from rocks and sand, and roji-tei, gardens built to accentuate the architecture of a teahouse.

京都では平安時代（794～1185年）から現代までの庭が鑑賞できる。日本庭園には各時代の思想や価値観が様式にも表現され、池を中心とした「池泉庭園」、石と砂で構成された「枯山水庭園」、茶室と合わせて造られた「露地庭」などが代表的だ。

Tenryu-ji Temple

天龍寺

The garden at Tenryu-ji Temple, founded in 1339, was designed by the Zen monk Muso Soseki, who was the first chief priest of the temple. This grand garden incorporates, or "borrows," scenery from the surrounding Arashiyama district.

1339年創建の天龍寺。禅宗の高僧・夢窓疎石の作庭は嵐山を借景とする雄大な庭だ。

☎ 075-881-1235 📍 P79-B3
🚶 Near Arashiyama Station on the Randen (Keifuku) line
[¥] 500yen (additional 100yen to enter the temple buildings)
🕐 8:30 – 17:30(Oct.21～Mar.20 -17:00)
📅 Open year round 7 days a week

There is a grouping of rocks toward the back of the pond that represents carp swimming up a waterfall.
池の奥には鯉が滝を登っている様子を表した石組みがある

Chisen-teien (pond garden)

池泉庭園

This style of garden features a pond surrounded by trees, plants and other natural elements, and it is thought to be one of the first types of Japanese garden. Varieties of chisen-teien include *kaiyu-shiki* (designed to be viewed while strolling around the pond), *kansho-shiki* (meant to be viewed from within temple buildings), and *senyu-shiki* (which are viewed from a boat in the pond).

池を中心とした豊かな自然があふれる庭園で日本庭園の原点となる形式。池の周りを歩きながら鑑賞する「回遊式」と、寺院の建物の室内から鑑賞する目的でつくられた「鑑賞式」、舟で池を巡る「舟遊式」などがある。

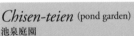

Borrowed scenery
借景

This is the practice of incorporating mountains and other landscape elements that exist outside the garden into the garden.

敷地外にある山並みなどの景色を庭の背景に取り入れること

Rock formations
石組み

Rocks are arranged to depict natural objects such as waterfalls, islands, and mountains.

石の組み合わせ方によって、滝、島、山などの自然物を表現

Pond
池

Ponds are placed in the heart of the garden. The water in the ponds comes from the Lake Biwa Canal and groundwater that flows down from the mountains around Kyoto.

池を中心に植え込みなどを配す。京都を囲む三方の山や琵琶湖疏水から流れる豊富な地下水を利用している

Never stray from the path in a kaiyu-shiki garden. Plants, moss and sand patterns can be damaged if stepped upon.

回遊式庭園では、苔などの植物や砂紋を踏むと庭が荒れてしまうため、通路以外を歩かないように。

Breathtaking colored leaves reflected on the surface of the pond in autumn.
秋には池の水面に見事な紅葉が映し出される

Kodai-ji Temple 高台寺

This garden was built around two ponds, Garyuchi and Engetsuchi. Visitors will find impressive rock formations that depict islands such as Tsurushima, in the form of a crane, and can also see the Kangetsudai, a platform designed for viewing the moon reflected in the water's surface at night.

臥龍池と偃月池を中心とする庭園には鶴島などの見事な石組みや、池に映る月を眺めるための観月台などが配されている。

☎075-561-9966 ♀P80-C3
🚶5 minute walk from the Kyoto City Bus Higashiyama-yasui bus stop 〔¥〕600yen (includes admission fee for the Sho Museum)
🕘9:00 – 17:00 (Subject to change depending on the season)
💺Open year round 7 days a week

The large stone in the middle of the pond looks like the back of a dragon that has dived into the water.
中央の巨石は水にもぐった龍の背のように見える

Shoren-in Monzeki Temple 青蓮院門跡

This temple traces its origins to the priest Saicho, the founder of the Tendai sect of Buddhism. It is thought that the garden was designed by the artist Soami (died 1525) and the pond, called Ryushinchi, has a stone bridge and waterfall.

天台宗の開祖・最澄の僧坊が起原の寺院。絵師・相阿弥（不明～1525）作と伝わる庭園の龍心池には石橋や滝が配される。

☎075-561-2345
♀P80-C2
🚶5 minute walk from Higashiyama Station on the Tozai subway line 〔¥〕500yen
🕘9:00 – 17:00 💺Open year round 7 days a week

Toji-in Temple 等持院

This was the family temple of the Ashikaga shoguns during the Muromachi period (1338-1573). The pond in the eastern part of the garden is called Shinji-ike, and the pond in the western part is called Fuyochi. Some say that these "stroll gardens" were designed by Muso Soseki.

☎075-461-5786
♀P78-B2
🚶7 minute walk from Toji-in Station on the Randen (Keifuku) line 〔¥〕500yen
🕘9:00 – 16:30
💺Open year round 7 days a week

室町幕府足利歴代将軍の菩提寺。心字池（東側）、芙蓉池（西側）を配した庭は、ともに回遊式庭園で夢窓疎石作庭という説も。

Trees, plants and flowers surround these east and west ponds, offering something to please the eye all year round.
東西の池の周囲にはさまざまな樹木や花が植えられ一年を通して楽しめる

The 15 rocks in this rectangular garden of white sand are placed so that a viewer can never see all 15 at once, no matter where they stand. The number 15 symbolizes fullness, and this garden is said to represent the Zen philosophy of always striving to reach such a state.
長方形に敷かれた白砂の上に15個の石が配されているが、どの角度からも一度に全ての石を見ることができない。15を「満」とし、常に「満」を目指すという禅の精神を説いているといわれる

Refresh your body and soul
✿ 心と体をリフレッシュ

Zen is a short form of "the Zen sect" and sometimes refers to zazen (seated meditation). The practice of zazen is considered the most important discipline in Zen Buddhism. Through it, practitioners seek to attain enlightenment by reflecting on their true nature just as the Buddha did. In around the 13th century, Zen became popular among the warrior class and the general populace alike. The Zen practice of calming the mind is reflected in various aspects of Japanese culture, from gardens to the tea ceremony.

禅は「禅宗」の略であり、坐禅を指すこともある。釈迦が悟りを開いた坐禅を最も重要な修行とし、坐禅の目的は "ありのままの自分と向き合う" こと。13世紀ごろ、武士や庶民にも広く浸透した。心を鎮める禅の教えは、庭園や茶道などをはじめ、日本文化の随所に反映されている。

○ **Ryoan-ji Temple**
龍安寺
☎075-463-2216 ♥P78-A2
♪ Near the Kyoto City Bus Ryoanji-mae
bus stop ｜¥500yen ⏰8:00－17:00
(8:30－16:30 from Dec. to Feb.)
⊛Open year round 7 days a week

Karesansui garden
(Dry landscape garden)
枯山水庭園

This type of garden depicts mountains and bodies of water in nature with rocks, sand, moss and other materials, but without actually using water. One of the most famous examples is the rock garden at Ryoan-ji Temple.

水を用いずに、石や砂、苔などを用いてそれらを山や川、海などに見立て、自然を表現する庭園形式。龍安寺石庭が代表格。

Zazen
(Seated meditation)
坐禅

Zazen is designed to help purify the soul through reflection upon one's true nature. If you begin to slouch while in zazen, you will be admonished by the monk with a sharp swat on the shoulder with a flat wooden stick called a keisaku.

自分自身と向き合い、心を清浄にする修行。姿勢が乱れると「警策」という棒状の板で肩を打たれ戒めを受ける。

○ **Nanzen-ji Temple, Ryuenkaku**
南禅寺 龍淵閣
☎075-771-0365 ♀P70-D3
🚶10 minute walk from Keage Station on the Tozai subway line
[¥]Free ⏱6:00 – 7:00 every 2nd and 4th Sunday (6:30 – 7:30 from Nov. to Mar.) ⊗No sessions held in Aug., on 2nd Sunday of Jan., or on 4th Sunday of Dec.

Doing zazen 坐禅の流れ

You are taught the correct sitting, leg and hand positions, and how to breathe.
姿勢、足や手の組み方、呼吸法を教えてもらう

Prepare your body, breathing and mind, and attempt to reflect on your true nature.
身体・呼吸・心を整え、自己と向き合う

If you are struck with the *keisaku*, bow once in return.
警策で戒めてもらったら一礼を忘れずに

Shakyo
(Transcribing sutras)
写経

Buddhist scriptures are written completely in Chinese characters, and the act of transcribing these texts is considered a form of spiritual training. Nowadays, many devotees engage in such training in order to have wishes fulfilled.

全て漢字で記された仏教経典を書き写す、禅修行の一つ。現代では、願掛けを目的として行う場合が多い。

○ **Nanzen-in, sub-temple of Nanzen-ji Temple**
南禅寺 南禅院
☎075-771-0365 ♀P70-D3
🚶10 minute walk from Keage Station on the Tozai subway line
[¥]1,000yen ⏱13:00 – 15:00 on the 15th of each month (It takes about 40 to 60 minutes to complete) ⊗No sessions held in Aug.

How to transcribe a sutra 写経の流れ

Listen to the sutras, the sermon, and the instructions on how to mentally prepare.
お坊さんの読経と法話、事前の心構えを聞く

As you carefully transcribe the characters, one by one, you will find your mind becomes calm.
一文字一文字丹念に書いていくと、いつの間にか心穏やかに

When complete, you place your transcription before the Buddha and begin to pray.
書き終えた写経を仏前に奉納し、祈願する

Religious Worship

| おまいり |

Worshipping at shrines and temples

✿ 神社や寺院の参拝の仕方

Worship in Japan comes in two forms. At shrines, visitors pray to the gods enshrined within. At temples, visitors greet the Buddha or Boddisattva to whom the temple is dedicated. There are specific rituals and etiquette required for each, so it's best to learn them ahead of time.

おまいりとは、神社では神、寺院では仏を拝む（もしくは祈る）行為。それぞれに正しい手順と作法があるので、マナーをしっかりと予習しておこう。

General etiquette 一般的な参拝方法

Chozuya:
The pavilion containing basins filled with pure water.

手水舎：清浄な水が満たされた水盤

Purify yourself at the chozuya

手水舎（ちょうずや）で清める

① Hold a ladle with your right hand and wash your left hand. ② Hold the ladle with your left hand and wash your right hand. ③ Hold the ladle with your right hand again, pour some water into your left hand and sip it to rinse your mouth. ④ Wash the left hand you just took a sip from. ⑤ Hold the ladle vertically so that the remaining water runs down the handle to purify it.

①柄杓を右手に持って左手を洗う ②次に柄杓を左手に持ちかえて右手を洗う ③右手に持ち替えた柄杓で左手に水を受け、口をすすぐ ④口を付けた左手を洗う ⑤柄杓を立てて柄杓を清める。

Make a monetary offering

お賽銭を納める

Osaisen refers to money offered upon worshipping. You gently toss the money into the offering box (*saisenbako*) installed there. Many people generally offer 5 to 100yen.

お賽銭とは、参拝する際に神様に奉納するお金のこと。設置されている箱（賽銭箱）へそっと入れる。金額はだいたい5〜100円が多い。

clap clap

⛩️At a Shinto shrine 神社の場合

Two bows, two claps, one bow

２拝２拍手１拝

Bow deeply twice, then clap your hands twice. Bring your palms together to quietly pray, then bow deeply once more. You should bow at an angle of around 90 degrees.

２回深くお辞儀をして２回拍手を打つ。手を合わせたまま静かに拝んだあと、再び１回深くお辞儀をする。お辞儀の角度は90度くらい。

Ringing the bell

鈴を鳴らす

Ring the bell or bells to let the god or Buddha know you have come to worship. Ringing loudly is thought to ward off evil.
(Procedures so far are common in shrines and temples.)

参拝に来たことを神仏に知らせる合図。力強く鳴らすことで邪気を祓う。（ここまでは神社も寺院も同じ）

🏯At a Buddhist temple 寺院の場合

One bow, palms together, and one bow

１拝手合わせ１拝

Bow deeply once then quietly pray with palms together. Unlike the procedure at shrines, worshippers do not clap their hands at temples. Bow deeply once more to finish.

１回深くお辞儀をして、手を合わせたまま静かに拝む。神社とは異なり、その際に拍手を打ってはいけない。最後にもう１回深くお辞儀をする。

25

Buddhist Statues

| 仏像 |

Four types of Buddhist statues

仏像の 4 つの種類

Japanese Buddha statues are classified into four types depending on their origin and characteristics, including hand gestures, items being carried, and clothing they are depicted as wearing.

仏像はその由来や性質から4つの位に分けられ、手指の形、持ち物、衣服などで見分けることができる。

Nyorai (Buddha) 如来
Bosatsu (Bodhisattva) 菩薩
Myo-o (Wisdom King) 明王
Tenbu (Deva) 天部

Nyorai (Buddha)　如来

Meaning "one who has attained enlightenment," this is the highest rank of being in the Buddhist Pantheon. The four primary Nyorai are Shaka Nyorai, Yakushi Nyorai, Amida Nyorai and Dainichi Nyorai. Depiction of Nyorai commonly show the hands held in a ritual gesture, or "*in.*"

「悟りの境地に達した者」を意味する最高位の存在。「釈迦如来」「薬師如来」「阿弥陀如来」「大日如来」の四如来が代表格。"印"と呼ばれる独特の手のポーズが特徴。

Bosatsu (Bodhisattva)　菩薩

These are practitioners who work hard to achieve enlightenment and become a Nyorai. Famous among them are Sho (Sacred) Kannon Bosatsu, Senju (Thousand-armed) Kannon Bosatsu, Miroku Bosatsu and Juichimen (Eleven-headed) Kannon Bosatsu. They wear elegant clothes and gorgeous accessories such as a crown and necklace.

「悟りを開き、如来になろうと励む修行者」。「聖観音菩薩」「千手観音菩薩」「弥勒菩薩」「十一面観音菩薩」などが有名。宝冠や首飾りなど豪華な装飾品に、優雅な衣服をまとう。

Learning about Buddhist statues

✿ 仏像彫刻を学ぶ

Buddhist statues are objects of devotion and include images of the Buddha and boddhisattvas. Usually made of metal, stone or wood, they also attract attention as beautiful artworks. Visiting Kyoto's temples will give you a sense of the wide variety of Buddhist statues that exist.

仏像とは、仏教を開いた仏陀（ブッダ）をはじめ、礼拝や信仰の対象となる仏や菩薩の像のことをいい、材質は金属、石、木などさまざま。その造形美が芸術品としても注目を集めている。京都の寺院を巡って色々な種類の仏像に会いに行こう。

Toji Temple
(Kyo-o-gokoku-ji Temple)
東寺（教王護国寺）

Toji Temple was built in 796 to guard the nation. With the Kodo Hall housing groups of Buddhist statues, three-dimensional mandala and other significant objects, the temple is said to be a treasure trove of Buddhist art. Standing approximately 55m high, the five-story wooden pagoda is the tallest in Japan and one of Kyoto's most famous landmarks.

東寺は国家鎮護のために796年に建立。講堂内には仏像群・立体曼荼羅があり、密教美術の宝庫といわれる。約55mと日本一の高さの木造の五重塔は、京都を代表するランドマーク。

☎075-691-3325 ♀P72-B3
🚶10 minute walk from Toji Station on the Kintetsu line
💰Free (500 yen to enter the Kondo and Kodo Halls)
🕐8:30-last admission 17:00 (last admission 16:00 from Sep. 20 to Mar. 19)
📅Open year round 7 days a week

Tenbu (Deva)　天部

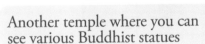

The Tenbu are a group of celestial beings that serve as protectors of Nyorai, Bosatsu and Myo-o. They come from various walks of life, some being warlords or members of the nobility, for example, and appear in numerous forms with a variety of facial expressions. They are considered to derive from gods that appear in ancient Indian myths.

「如来、菩薩、明王を護る神のグループ」。武将や貴人などさまざまな出自を反映し、姿や顔立ちも多種多様。インドで古くから神話などに登場する神が由来と考えられる。

Another temple where you can see various Buddhist statues

さまざまな仏像に出会える寺院

Sanjusangen-do Temple　三十三間堂

The main hall of Sanjusangen-do Temple is the longest wooden structure in Japan. It holds 1,000 statues of the Senju Kannon, the 1000-armed depiction of the boddhisattva who symbolizes compassion. They each were given different expressions and clothing, and display 11 faces atop their heads and 40 arms stretching from their sides.

日本一長い木造建築物である本堂には、1000体の等身大千手観音立像が、整然と並ぶ。1体ずつ表情、装飾が違い、頭上に11面の顔を持ち、両脇から40の手が伸びる。

☎075-561-0467　♀P73-E2　🚶Near the Kyoto City Bus Hakubutsukan-Sanjusangen-do-mae bus stop　💰600yen
🕐8:00-17:00 (9:00-16:00 from Nov. 16 to Mar. 31. Admission up to 30 minutes before closing time)
📅Open year round 7 days a week

Myo-o (Wisdom King)　明王

Myo-o are beings who have gained the wisdom of a Buddha. They are an incarnation of Dainichi Nyorai and strike fear into those who do not adhere to the teachings. They are usually depicted with flames emanating behind them, hair standing on end and a ferocious eye-bulging expression that suggests with their entire body the extent of their wrath.

「仏の智恵を習得した者」。大日如来の化身で、教えに逆らう者を懲らしめる。火炎を背負い、髪を逆立て目をむいた恐ろしい顔つきで、全身で怒りを表した姿のものが多い。

⑫ Omikuji ｜おみくじ｜

Learning your fortune
❀ 吉凶を占う

Omikuji are small pieces of paper on which your fortune is written, and they are available at shrines and temples. In Japan, many people draw an omikuji every time they go to worship. Fortunes are described as blessings (kichi) or curses (kyo), and they contain advice regarding things such as health, love, study and business.

おみくじとは、運勢が記された小さな紙のことで、神社や寺院で授与されている。日本ではおまいりする度におみくじを引く人が多い。運勢は「吉」と「凶」に分けて表され、健康・恋愛・学問・商売など項目立ててアドバイスが書かれている。

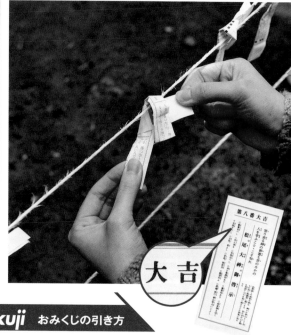

How to draw an Omikuji　おみくじの引き方

1 Draw a lottery stick
くじを引く

Shake the cylinder that contains the lottery sticks while praying to the god or Buddha of the institution you are visiting. Turn the box upside down to allow a stick to drop out through the small hole and check the number written on it.

神仏に祈願し神聖な気持ちで棒の入った筒を振る。筒を逆さにすると小さな穴から1本の棒が出てくるので、そこに刻まれた番号を確認する。

2 Pay the fee
お金を払う

Tell a shrine attendant your number, and then pay for the omikuji corresponding to that number. Open the paper up and carefully read it.

神社の人に番号を伝え、その番号のおみくじを受け取り、代金を支払う。おみくじを開封し、書かれた内容をよく読む。

3 Tie it to a tree branch
木に結ぶ

Tie your omikuji to a tree branch (or other designated place). It is believed that tying it to a tree branch imbues it with the life force of the tree, enabling your wish to come true.

木の枝（または所定の場所）におみくじを結び付ける。木の枝に結ぶことで樹木の生命力を得て、願い事が叶うとされる。

28

The ice which covered the pond has melted away in the spring sun. The flowers are reflecting their shadows on the water.

Your Fortune	Quite Good

Just like flowers are in full bloom on a warm spring day, you can get rid of the troubles you've suffered from. Behave yourself and love others and be faithful, and you'll be happier.

■ **wish** : Everything goes as you wish, but don't go to extremes.
■ **expected visitor** : He(or she) will come, but late.
■ **missing thing** : It will surely be found. Look for it between things.
■ **travel** : Take it easy.

■ **business** : It's time to sell. You'll get profit.
■ **study** : Banish worldly thoughts from your mind. Study hard.
■ **speculation** : Sell it now, or you'll lose.
■ **game and match** : You will win completely.
■ **love** : Trust him(or her). He is a very good person.
■ **removal** : The sooner, the better.
■ **childbirth** : Easy. Both a mother and a baby will be well.
■ **illness** : Consult a good doctor, and you'll be cured.
■ **marriage proposal** : Just keep it secret, or there will be some troubles.

How to read your fortune
運勢の見分け方

大吉 Great blessing (Dai-kichi)
Extremely good and couldn't be better
絶好調、これ以上ないくらいよい、すばらしい

Kichi fortunes represent happiness and are classified from highest to lowest as dai, chu, sho, and sue.
幸運を意味し、大・中・小・末などとランクに分かれて表される。一般的には大吉が最も幸運。

吉 Blessing (Kichi)
Very good とてもよい

小吉 Small blessing (Sho-kichi)
Not bad ちょっとよい

中吉 Middle blessing (Chu-kichi)
Good よい

末吉 Ending blessing (Sue-kichi)
Not very bad ほんの少しよいかもしれない

凶 Curse (Kyo)
Bad 悪い

A kyo result is thought to mean that you have bad luck, while dai-kyo means that your luck couldn't be any worse. Some think that getting dai-kyo simply means that things can only get better.
凶とは運が悪い状態。大凶だと最悪という意味。ただし一番悪ければ、その後は運気上がるのみ、という考え方がある。

大凶 Great curse (Dai-kyo)
Very bad とても悪い

★★★★★★★★★★★★★★
★ A★Written Oracle ★
★★★★★★★★★★★★★★ No.28

Your fortune 運勢

Unique *omikuji* ユニークなおみくじ

Omikuji (English)
おみくじ(英文) 100yen

Nonomiya-jinja Shrine
野宮神社

This shrine is popular for its god of matchmaking. Just put money in the box and draw an omikuji.
縁結びの神様として人気の神社。箱にお金を入れてからおみくじを引く。

☎075-871-1972 ♀P79-B3
🚶11 minute walk from Saga-arashiyama Station on the JR line
[¥] Free ⏰9:00 – 17:00
📅Open year round 7 days a week

Kofuku Hato-mikuji
幸福鳩みくじ 500yen

Rokkaku-do Temple (Choho-ji Temple)
六角堂(頂法寺)

The omikuji here comes with an unglazed ceramic dove, a symbol of happiness that you can take home with you.
幸せの象徴・白い鳩の素焼きに付いたおみくじ。鳩は持ち帰れる。

☎075-221-2686 ♀P74-C2
🚶3 minute walk from Karasuma-oike Station on the Karasuma & Tozai subway line
[¥] Free ⏰6:00-17:00 📅Open year round 7 days a week

Karakuri Omikuji (English)
からくりおみくじ(英文) 200yen

Nishiki Tenman-gu Shrine
錦天満宮

With this gimmicky *omikuji* machine, a lion doll presents you with an omikuji as it does the *shishimai* lion dance.
機械仕掛けのからくりおみくじ。獅子頭が踊りながらおみくじを引き授与してくれる。

☎075-231-5732 ♀P75-D3
🚶3 minute walk from Kawaramachi Station on the Hankyu line [¥] Free
⏰8:00 (gate opened) – 20:00 (gate closed)
📅Open year round 7 days a week

The English translations appearing on omikuji may vary by venue.

運勢の英語表記はおみくじによって異なる場合があります。

En-musubi ｜縁結び｜

Shrines known for love
✿縁結びで評判の神社

In Japan, visiting temples and shrines is said to influence one's life in a positive way. Some of the most popular among women are those which offer success in romance, whether one is seeking the return of unrequited love or a stronger relationship with a current partner.

神社や寺には、いろいろな御利益がある。なかでも女性に人気なのが縁結び。片思いの相手を想ったり、恋人同士のさらなる愛の発展を願ったり、恋愛成就のさまざまな願い事を叶えてくれる。

Where is the other stone?
石はどこかな〜？

The Love Stones
Jishu-jinja Shrine

恋占いの石〈地主神社〉

This famous shrine is dedicated to a god of love, and people searching for a partner come here to pray. The "love stones" located here, which are about 10 meters apart, are said to grant that wish if a visitor can walk from one to the other with their eyes closed.

縁結びの神様として有名な神社。恋人が欲しい人がおまいりに来る。境内にある、10mほど離れた2つの石の間を、目を閉じたまま歩いてたどり着くことができると、恋が叶うといわれる。

☎075-541-2097 ♥P80-C4
🚶10 minute walk from the Kyoto City Bus Gojo-zaka or Kiyomizu-michi bus stop
[¥]Free (400yen required to enter Kiyomizu-dera Temple)
⏱9:00-17:00 📅Open year round 7 days a week

This time, I'm wishing for a good relationship!
今回は良縁祈願♥

The Separation & Matchmaking monument
Yasui Konpira-gu Shrine
縁切り縁結び碑〈安井金比羅宮〉

The power of the deities enshrined here flows through the tunnel in the center of this monument. Crawling through from front to back helps end bad relationships, and crawling through in the other direction helps start good relationships. Visitors write their names and prayers upon paper charms called katashiro (for which you pay as you wish) which are then affixed to the monument.

碑には神様の力が注ぎこむという穴があり、表から裏へ抜けると悪縁を切り、裏から表に抜けると良縁を結ぶことで有名。碑には、願い事と名前を書いた紙のお札 "形代"（志納）を貼る。

This is the front side
こちらが表

☎075-561-5127 ♀P80-B3
🚶3 minute walk from the Kyoto City Bus Higashiyama Yasui bus stop
[¥] 🕐 Free and always open to the public
📅 Open year round 7 days a week

Unique Omamori(amulets)　ユニークなお守り

Omamori are charms you carry on your person to receive divine protection. They include charms for good health, traffic safety and easy birth. They come in a variety of colors and shapes and also make good gifts.
加護を願い、身に着けるもの。「無病息災」「交通安全」「安産祈願」など、ご利益はさまざまで、色や形も豊富だ。プレゼントにもなる。

Good luck 開運
Katsu-mamori
Seimei-jinja Shrine
勝守〈晴明神社〉　600yen

These amulets are carried by people hoping for a "win" in a test or sporting event. The pentagram wards off evil, and is also the symbol of Abe-no-seimei, the legendary figure enshrined here.
試験やスポーツに "勝つ" ためのお守り。魔除けを意味する五芒星は祭神・安倍晴明（陰陽師）が発案した紋だ。

☎ 075-441-6460 ♀P76-B3
🚶 2 minute walk from the Kyoto City Bus Ichijo-modoribashi, Seimei-jinja-mae bus stop
[¥] Free 🕐 9:00-18:00
📅 Open year round 7 days a week

Economic fortune 金運
Icho amulet
Mikane-jinja Shrine
いちょう守〈御金神社〉　1,000yen

This gold-colored amulet is in the shape of a gingko leaf, the gingko tree being the sacred tree of the shrine and thought to increase economic fortune.
金運を上げるご利益があるご神木・イチョウの葉をかたどった黄金色のお守り。

☎075-222-2062 ♀P74-C2 🚶 5 minute walk from Karasuma Oike Station on the Karasuma subway line
[¥] 🕐 Free and always open to the public 📅 Open year round 7 days a week

Matchmaking 縁結び
Aoi-mamori
Shimogamo-jinja Shrine
葵守り〈下鴨神社〉　500yen

This motif is based on the heart-shaped leaves of the futaba-aoi, a plant featured in the shrine's crest. They are available in green or pink.
神社の御神紋、双葉葵という植物のハート型の葉がモチーフ。緑とピンクの2種類ある。

☎075-781-0010 ♀P77-E1
🚶 Near the Kyoto City Bus Shimogamo-jinja-mae bus stop
[¥]Free (Special viewing of Oidono Hall, Okurumaya and Kawai-jinja Shrine is 500yen for all)
🕐 6:30-17:00 (Special viewing 10:00-16:00)
📅 Open year round 7 days a week

Traffic safety 交通安全
"Safe Flight" amulet
Kamigamo-jinja Shinto Shrine
航空安全お守り〈上賀茂神社〉　800yen

This amulet is unusual for its stitched design of an airplane. It derives from the Yatagarasu, a crow that supposedly flies to lead travelers on their way.
飛行機が刺繍された珍しいお守り。空から旅人を先導するといわれている八咫烏が由来。

☎075-781-0011 ♀P70-C2
🚶 Near the Kyoto City Bus Kamiga-mojinja-mae bus stop
[¥]Free (500yen for special worshipping at the Honden and Gonden halls)
🕐 8:00-17:00 (8:30 - from Nov. to Mar., 10:00-16:00 for special worshipping, -16:30 on Saturdays, Sundays and holidays)
📅 Open year round 7 days a week

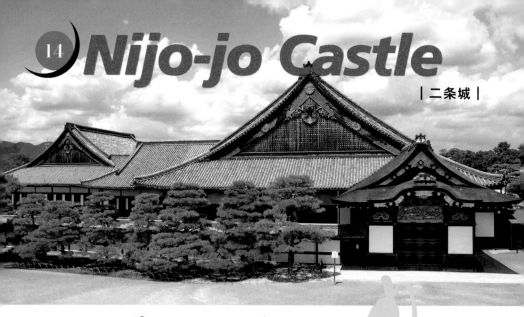

⑭ Nijo-jo Castle

| 二条城 |

A castle of majestic splendor

✿ 豪華絢爛を極めた城

This castle was built in 1603 by Tokugawa Ieyasu, the first shogun of the Tokugawa Shogunate, for the purpose of protecting the Kyoto Imperial Palace and also as his residence in Kyoto. It originally had a donjon, but it has since burned down. Defenses were incorporated into the design as can be seen by the respective moats around the entire perimeter and the Honmaru Palace. This is the only World Cultural Heritage site in Kyoto that is not a temple or shrine.

1603年、江戸幕府の初代将軍・徳川家康が京都御所の守護と京都の宿所として建てた城。かつては天守閣があったが焼失。敷地および本丸の周囲に堀を設けるなどの防護策が見受けられる。京都では社寺以外で唯一の世界文化遺産。

☎ 075-841-0096 ♀ P74-B1
🚶 Near the Kyoto City Bus Nijo-jo-mae bus stop
¥ 600yen
🕐 8:45-17:00 (last admission 16:00, Ninomaru Palace from 9:00-16:00)
📅 Tuesdays in Jan., Jul., Aug. and Dec. (or Wednesday when Tuesday is a national holiday)

The Tokugawa Shogunate
徳川将軍

Victory in battle in 1600 made Tokugawa Ieyasu he preeminent samurai warrior of his time, and he assumed political control when the reigning Emperor appointed him to the position of shogun. For approximately 300 years, the Tokugawa family exerted dominant control over the country in what is called the Edo period, lasting from 1603 to 1868, when the 15th shogun, Yoshinobu, returned the reins of government to the Emperor.

1600年、合戦で勝利を納めた徳川家康が武士の首長となり、天皇より将軍に任命され政治の実権を握る。その後、1867年、15代将軍・慶喜が政権を天皇に返上するまでの約300年、徳川家を中心とした江戸時代（1603～1868）が続いた。

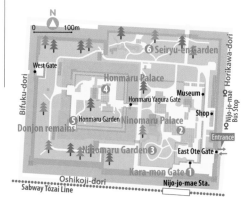

① Kara-mon Gate 唐門

This is the main gate of the Ninomaru Palace. It is impressive for the decorative sculpted lions, tigers, dragons and other motifs lavishly depicted in gold and sumptuous colors.

二の丸御殿の正門。金色と極彩色で唐獅子や虎、龍などの豪華な彫刻が施された装飾が見事。

② Ninomaru Palace 二の丸御殿

Covering an area of 3,300m², this magnificent structure has 33 rooms and consists of six connected buildings, including the Ohiroma (Great Hall), Kuro-shoin (Inner Audience Chamber) and Shiro-shoin (Shogun's living quarters). In the most official and formal Ohiroma hall, there are wall paintings by artists of the Kano school, known to many as the greatest school in the history of Japanese painting.

大広間、黒書院、白書院など6棟からなり、建物の総面積3300㎡、部屋数33と壮大な規模。最も公的で格式高い大広間には、日本絵画史上最大の流派・狩野派による障壁画が描かれている。

③ Ninomaru Garden 二の丸庭園

The garden took on its current state around the year 1626, after the third shogun, Tokugawa Iemitsu, commissioned garden designer Kobori Enshu to work on it. The pond has three islands, four bridges, and a two-tiered stone waterfall.

現在の姿は、3代将軍・徳川家光が作庭家・小堀遠州に命じ、1626年ごろ改修されたもの。池には3つの島が浮かび、4つの橋が架かり、二段の滝の石組みも配されている。

④ Honmaru Palace 本丸御殿

Featuring a spacious lawn-type garden in the foreground, this magnificent palace was brought here in 1893 from its original location on the grounds of the Kyoto Imperial Palace, where it was part of the imperial Katsura-no-miya family's residence. The interior is not open to the public.

広々とした芝庭風の庭園に立つ荘厳な御殿は、1893年、京都御苑にあった皇族・桂宮家の屋敷の一部を移築したもの。内部は非公開。

⑤ Donjon Remains 天守閣跡

There used to be a five-story donjon standing in the southwest corner of the Honmaru that was visible beyond the garden of the Ninomaru Palace. Only the walls have been preserved since it was struck by lightning and burned down. It now serves as a viewing platform.

本丸の西南角にはかつて五層の天守閣があり、二の丸御殿より庭園越しに眺められた。落雷により焼失して以降は石垣のみを残し、現在は展望台となっている。

⑥ Seiryu-en Garden 清流園

This garden was created in 1965 and is essentially a combination of two gardens. On the east side is a Western-style garden carpeted in grass, and on the west side is a Japanese stroll garden, creating a tasteful juxtaposition of East and West.

1965年に作られた庭園。東側に芝生を敷き詰めた洋風庭園、西側に池を配した和風の回遊式庭園と、和洋折衷の趣を感じられる。

Kyoto Imperial Palace

| 京都御所 |

The imperial symbol of the city

✿ 京都のランドマーク

Kyoto Imperial Palace is a special place where successive Emperors lived for about 500 years from the 14th century until 1869 when the capital was moved to Tokyo. Extant buildings include the *Shishin-den*, *Seiryo-den* and Kogosho. The current buildings were built in 1855.

御所とは、14世紀以来、1869年の東京遷都まで約500年間、歴代の天皇が暮らした特別な場所だ。紫宸殿や清涼殿、小御所などの御殿が現存する。現在の建物は1855年に造営された。

What does Tenno mean ? 天皇とは?

Tenno, or Emperor, is the title that has been given to the rulers of Japan since ancient times. The Japanese emperors lived in Kyoto during the time it was the country's capital, from 794 to 1869. The shoguns governed the country from their own lands, nominally appointed by the Emperor. The current Emperor is the 125th and is now considered a symbol of the state.

古代より続く日本の歴代の君主の称号。794年から1869年の間、京都を都として定め定住した。天皇に任命された将軍は、主たる領地において国を統治した。現在は「日本国の象徴」とされ、現天皇は第125代目。

○ ♀P77-D3
🚶 Near Marutamachi and Imadegawa Stations on the Karasuma subway line

Shishin-den:The Shishin-den is considered the most formal building on the palace grounds. It contains the *takamikura* Emperor's throne and was used to conduct imperial enthronements and other important ceremonies. Planted in the white gravel garden are the *Sakon-no-sakura* cherry tree on the east side and the *Ukon-no-tachibana* mandarin tree on the west side.

紫宸殿：御所内で最も格式が高いとされる建物。内部には高御座（玉座）が置かれ、天皇の即位式など重要な儀式が執り行われた。白砂の庭には東側に左近の桜、西側に右近の橘が植えられている。

Seiryo-den:The Emperors spent much of their daily lives in this building, which is characterized by a complex structure with many partitions.

清涼殿：天皇が日常生活を送っていた場所。間仕切りが多い複雑な構造になっている。

Kyoto Gyoen National Garden: (☎075-211-6348 [¥]Free ♀P77-D4) Itozakura cherry trees reach full bloom in spring at the garden , which surrounds the Kyoto Imperial Palace.

京都御苑：京都御所を取り囲む公園で春には糸桜が満開になる。

Other palace and villas
その他の御所&離宮

Sento Imperial Palace 仙洞御所

This palace of the Retired Emperor Go-mizunoo was completed in 1630. It was not rebuilt after being destroyed by fire in 1854, and all that remain today are some teahouses and the sprawling garden, which are designed around two large ponds.

1630年に後水尾上皇の御所として造営。御殿は1854年に焼失した後、再建されず、2つの大池を中心とした大庭園と茶室のみが残る。

📍P77-D4　🚶15 minute walk from Marutamachi Station on the Karasuma subway line

Katsura Imperial Villa
桂離宮

Katsura Imperial Villa was built in the early 17th century as a villa of Prince Toshihito, the first head of the Hachijo-no-miya family. Famously praised by the German architect Bruno Taut as being "so beautiful it makes me want to cry," the garden located on the villa's vast grounds features an elegant balance of pond and teahouses.

17世紀初期、八条宮家初代智仁親王が別荘として造営。広大な敷地に池や茶室がバランスよく配置された庭園は、ドイツの建築家ブルーノ・タウトが「泣きたくなるほど美しい」と絶賛したことで有名。

📍P71-B4　🚶8 minute walk from the Kyoto City Bus Katsura-rikyu-mae bus stop

Shugakuin Imperial Villa
修学院離宮

This is a hillside suite of buildings and gardens built by the Retired Emperor Go-Mizunoo in the middle of the 17th century. Containing a Lower, Middle and Upper Villa each with its own distinctive atmosphere, together they are in superb harmony with the lush natural surroundings. Any season is a great time to go enjoy the panoramic vista.

17世紀中ごろ、後水尾上皇により造営された山荘と庭園。敷地内に立つ上・中・下3つの趣が異なる造りの離宮と、緑豊かな自然の調和が見事。どの季節に訪れても味わい深いパノラマが楽しめる。

📍P70-D2　🚶15 minute walk from the Kyoto City Bus Shugakuin-rikyu-michi bus stop

Making reservations to visit Kyoto's Imperial Properties
参拝申込ガイド

見学無料 ※参観は事前申込が必要
（参観希望日の3カ月前の月の1日より申し込み可能）

Kyoto Imperial Palace / Sento Imperial Palace
Katsura Imperial Villa / Shugakuin Imperial Villa
☎ 075-211-1215 (Imperial Household Agency Kyoto Office)
[¥] Free　*Application in advance is required for visiting these sites. (Applications are accepted from the 1st day of the month three months before the month in which you wish to schedule your visit.)
http://sankan.kunaicho.go.jp/english/index.html

16) Arashiyama | 嵐山 |

Enjoy scenic beauty
✿ 風光明媚な景色を堪能

Approximately 1,000 years ago, aristocrats would build resort villas in this lush natural environment. The Togetsu-kyo Bridge and Chikurin-no-michi (Bamboo Forest Path) are just some of Arashiyama's iconic and highly recommended tourist sites. One great idea would be to begin a stroll from Arashiyama Station on the Randen (Keifuku) line: you could visit a temple and gardens, and then perhaps make your way to the open-sided Romantic Train for a scenic ride, or even take a boat ride down the Hozugawa River. Come for the Sakura in spring and the autumn colors in fall.

約1000年前、貴族たちの別荘地だった自然豊かな場所。渡月橋や竹林の道など嵐山を代表する景観は必見。嵐電嵐山駅を出発し、寺院や庭園を見学しながらそぞろ歩きを楽しみ、トロッコ列車や保津川下りも体験できるおすすめコースを紹介。春は桜、秋は紅葉が楽しめる。

P79-B3　🚶 5 minute walk from Arashiyama Station on the Randen (Keifuku) line
💴 🕐 🈺 Open to the public

It's also a famous photo spot
記念撮影スポットとしても有名

Chikurin-no-michi
竹林の道

This path is 400 meters long, starting at Nonomiya-jinja Shrine and continuing on to Okochi Sanso Garden. The path is lined on both sides by green bamboo trees between five and ten meters tall. This mysterious path provides cool, refreshing relief even in summer.

野宮神社から大河内山荘庭園まで約400m続く道。両脇に高さ5〜10mの青々とした竹が生い茂る。夏でもひんやりと空気が澄んでいる神秘的な道だ。

Arashiyama Station on the Randen (Keifuku) line 嵐電嵐山駅
🚩 **Start**

Short walk
徒歩すぐ

Tenryu-ji Temple
天龍寺（→P20）

Unryu-zu (Cloud Dragon) painted on the ceiling of the Hatto (Dharma Hall)
法堂の天井に描かれた雲龍図

10 minute walk
徒歩10分

Short walk
徒歩すぐ

Nonomiya-jinja Shrine
野宮神社（→P29）

People come here to pray for luck in love. The shrine appears in *the Tale of Genji*, a piece of classical Japanese literature written in the Heian period.

縁結びの祈願スポット。平安時代の日本古典文学『源氏物語』にも登場する神社。

Rare example of a dark-colored torii gate with bark on the poste.
木の皮を剥かずにつくられた珍しい黒木鳥居

Sagano Romantic Train

嵯峨野トロッコ列車

This popular sightseeing train gives a stunning view of Hozukyo Gorge, and it takes approximately 25 minutes to travel the 7.3 km between Torokko Saga and Torokko Kameoka stations.
All seats are reserved and we recommend you make your reservation in advance of your visit.

トロッコ嵯峨駅～トロッコ亀岡駅間 7.3㎞を約 25 分で走る人気の観光列車で、保津峡の絶景を眺められる。座席は全席指定席のため事前予約したほうがよい。

Encounter breathtaking valleys, forests and other beautiful natural scenery.
渓谷や森林の美しい自然風景に出合うことができる

☎075-861-7444 Sagano Scenic Railway (automated phone system) ♀P79-B・C3 🚶Near Saga-arashiyama Station on the JR line [¥]Fare: 620yen for one way ⏱ 🌐 http://www.sagano-kanko.co.jp/english.php

> 1 minute walk
> To Torokko Arashiyama Station
> トロッコ嵐山駅まで
> 徒歩 1 分

> Approximately a 25-minute ride on the Romantic Train
> トロッコで約 25 分

Stroll through this immense, 20,000m² garden.
約 2 万㎡の広大な回遊式庭園を散策できる

Okochi Sanso Garden

大河内山荘庭園

This villa and garden belonged to Denjiro Okochi, a big star of samurai films who was active in the early 20th century. *Matcha* and sweets are served at the rest house.

20 世紀前半に活躍した時代劇映画の大スター・大河内傳次郎の別荘庭園。休憩所では抹茶とお菓子のサービスも。

> Short walk
> 徒歩すぐ

☎075-872-2233 ♀P79-B3
🚶10 minute walk from the Kyoto City Bus Nonomiya bus stop [¥]1,000yen (including *matcha* and sweets) ⏱9:00 – 17:00 🌐Open year round 7 days a week

> The boat ride takes approximately 2hours
> 船下り約 2 時間

> Start

Hozugawa River Boat Ride

保津川下り

The 16 km ride down the river takes about two hours, and guests will experience both rapids and calm waters. The boatmen steer the boats with incredible skill.

約 16 km を約 2 時間かけて急流と穏やかな流れを越えていく船下り。船頭さんの巧みな竿さばきにも注目だ。

Be ready to get a little wet!
水しぶきを浴びることも

Feel the pulse of nature throughout your body in this magnificent gorge
雄大な渓谷の自然を間近に体感できる

☎0771-22-5846 ♀P79-B4
🚶15 minute ride on the Keihan Kyoto Kotsu Bus from Torokko Kameoka Station [¥]Fare: 4,100yen
⏱ 🌐 http://www.hozugawakudari.jp/en

Hozugawa River Boat Ride boat slip (near Togetsu-kyo Bridge)
保津川下り着船場（渡月橋付近）
Goal

Map:
Jojakko-ji Temple
to Saga-Arashiyama Sta.
Nonomiya-jinja Shrine
to Torokko Hozu-kyo Sta.
Okochi Sanso Garden
Sagano Romantic Train
Torokko Arashiyama Sta.
Chikurin-no Michi
Arashiyama Garden
Tenryu-ji Temple
Randen (Keifuku)line Arashiyama Sta.
29
Hozugawa River
Togetsu-kyo
N
0 200m

Arashiyama Monkey Park Iwatayama

| 嵐山モンキーパークいわたやま |

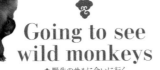

Going to see wild monkeys

✿ 野生のサルに会いに行く

About 120 Japanese macaques live in this wild-monkey park located on Mt. Iwatayama, a branch peak of Mt. Arashiyama. Although they are wild monkeys, they are fed for the purpose of promoting local tourism, and each one of them is identifiable and has its own name. When you visit, you can take photos with the monkeys and try feeding them yourself.

嵐山の支峰・岩田山にある野猿公園で、約120頭のニホンザルが暮らす。元来、地元の観光振興のために餌付けされたため、野生ではあるが、今もすべてのサルに名前が付いて判別できる。えさやり体験やサルと一緒に記念撮影ができる。

You will see a long slide and monkeys.
長い滑り台とサルが見えてくる

\ GOAL /

There are quizzes related to monkeys at a few locations in the park.
数か所でサルにまつわるクイズができる

Climb up these few hundred steps.
数百段ある長い階段を登る

The Monkey Park reception desk will come into view on your left.
左手にモンキーパークの受付がみえる

Climb up the steps of Ichitani-munakata-jinja Shrine.
櫟谷宗像神社の階段を登る

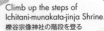

Togetsu-kyo Bridge
渡月橋

Arashiyama Station
on the Randen (Keifuku) line
嵐電嵐山駅

\ START /

Take some commemorative photos!
記念撮影できますよ!

\Say cheese/

Arashiyama Monkey Park Iwatayama

About a 20 minute stroll through the forest will bring you from the reception desk to the park at the top.

受付から約20分、森林の中を登ると山頂のパークに到着

Viewing platform
展望台

The monkey-feeding area and viewing platform are located at the top of this 160m mountain. It commands a panoramic view of Kyoto City, with its cherry blossoms in spring and colored leaves in autumn. Ask the staff to help call the monkeys over so you can take some commemorative photos.

標高160mの山頂にあるサルのえさ場兼展望台。京都市内を一望でき、春は桜、秋は紅葉の美しい風景が楽しめる。スタッフに頼めば、サルと一緒に記念撮影できるよう、サルの呼び寄せを手伝ってくれる。

☎075-872-0950 ♀P79-B4
🚶10 minute walk (to the reception desk) from Arashiyama Station on the Randen (Keifuku) line
[¥]550yen
🕘9:00-17:30 (last admission 17:00), 9:00-16:30 (last admission 16:00) from Oct. 10 to Mar. 14
Open year round 7 days a week

Be careful not to let the monkeys grab the whole bag from you.
サルにエサ袋ごと取られることもあるので要注意

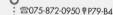

Give me some more!
もっとちょうだい〜

Feeding
えさやり

You can feed the monkeys from inside the hut on top of the mountain (100yen for a bag of peanuts or apples). At this park, it's the people who are fenced off, not the monkeys.

山頂にある休憩所の中からエサやり体験(1袋100円、リンゴか落花生)ができる。ここではサルではなく人間が金網の中に入る。

18 Kamogawa River

| 鴨川 |

See where Kyoto residents come to relax and take in the surroundings

✿ 市民の憩いの場で自然を体感しよう

Nature abounds on the banks of the Kamogawa River, the clear waters of which run from north to south through Kyoto. Many of Kyoto's residents come to walk, jog or cycle. It's the perfect place to come for a leisurely stroll during your sightseeing.

A "flower corridor" exists between the Sanjo-ohashi Bridge and Shichijo-ohashi Bridges where weeping willows and cherry trees present a splendid contrast in spring. Egrets (left), mallards (right) and other wild birds can be seen here.

三条大橋〜七条大橋間はシダレヤナギと桜が植えられた「花の回廊」では、春になるとコントラストが見事。シラサギ（左）、マガモ（右）などの野鳥も見られる

京都の街中を北から南へ流れる鴨川は、清冽な水が流れ、自然豊かな河畔が広がっている。散歩やジョギング、サイクリングなどを楽しむ市民も多い。観光の合間にしばしゆったりと散策してみよう。

P77-E3
Near Demachi-yanagi Station on the Keihon line

The raised river delta and Tadasu-no-mori grove at Shimogamo-Jinja Shrine can be seen From Kamo-ohashi Bridge.
賀茂大橋からデルタと下鴨神社の糺の森が見渡せる

The Greatest Travel Tips Kyoto

Stepping stones 飛び石

Near Kamo-ohashi Bridge, the east and west banks of the river are joined by steppingstones in the shape of turtles and plovers providing a fun way to get across.

賀茂大橋付近にある千鳥や亀の形をしている飛び石が川の東西を結んでいるので渡ってみよう。

> Turn back the rocks on the riverbank to find crayfish or mud snails underneath them.
> 川岸の岩をめくると裏側にザリガニやタニシがいる。

Grass lawn 芝生

You can come to read or have a picnic on the grass lawn of the raised delta where there is a convergence of two rivers.

2つの川に挟まれた三角州周辺に芝生が広がり本を読んだりピクニックをすることも。

> *Kojin-bashi Bridge*: Every spring, mallard families leave nearby temple ponds and come to the Kamogawa River.
> 荒神橋：毎年春にカモの親子が近くの寺院の池から鴨川にお引越し。

Noryo-yuka (Open-air riverbed dining terrace) 納涼床

From May to September, you can enjoy eating and drinking on the Noryo-yuka terraces set up by approximately 300 restaurants along the river between Sanjo Street and Gojo Street.

5～9月は三条通から五条通間の川沿いの約300軒の飲食店が設置した納涼床で飲食を楽しめる。

Cycling サイクリング

There is a path about 5km long from Shichijo-ohashi Bridge to Shimogamo-jinja Shrine on which you can enjoy cycling.

七条大橋付近から下鴨神社周辺まで約5kmほどの遊歩道が続き、サイクリングができる。

> When you have food, watch out for kites swooping down to steal it!
> 食べ物を持っているトンビが奪いにくるので要注意。

Couples カップル

The riverbank is also a popular place to come and sit during a date. It's a little amusing to see how equally the couples manage to space themselves out!

鴨川に沿って等間隔にカップルが座っている姿がおもしろい。デートスポットでもある。

Statues 像

At the Gojo-ohashi Bridge, Shijo-ohashi Bridge and other bridges, there are statues of historical figures who have some kind of link to the location.

五条大橋、四条大橋などには、その地に縁のある歴史的人物をモチーフにした像が点在する。

Demachi-bashi Bridge 出町橋
Delta デルタ
Kawai-bashi Bridge 河合橋
出町柳
Kamo-ohashi Bridge 賀茂大橋
Demachiyanagi Sta.
Kojin-bashi Bridge 荒神橋
Marutamachi-bashi Bridge 丸太町橋
神宮丸太町
Jingu-marutamachi Sta.
Nijo-ohashi Bridge 二条大橋
Oike-ohashi Bridge 御池大橋
三条
Sanjo Sta.
Sanjo-ohashi Bridge 三条大橋
祇園四条
Gion-shijo Sta.
Shijo-ohashi Bridge 四条大橋
清水五条
Kiyomizu-gojo st.
Gojo-ohashi Bridge 五条大橋
Keihan line 京阪電車

Samurai and Ninja

| サムライと忍者 |

The Heroes of Japan

✿ 日本のヒーロー

The samurai and the ninja are popular characters in Japanese period dramas. One with the trademark top-knot and swords belted to the waist, the other dressed in black and in a mask, using throwing stars and the art of *ninjutsu* to overcome opponents. There are two popular spots in Kyoto where tourists can meet up with such characters.

個性的な髪型のチョンマゲと腰に差した刀がトレードマークの侍と、黒装束の覆面姿で、飛び道具・手裏剣や忍法を用いて敵に挑む忍者は、日本の時代劇の人気キャラクター。京都で侍と忍者に出合える2つの人気エンタメスポットに行ってみよう。

Jidaigeki, Behind-The-Scenes

Chambara

チャンバラ 辻指南
See the samurai put on an impressive display of their sword-fighting skills. Audience members can also take part. (4 times a day, 15 minutes long)
迫力たっぷりの"チャンバラ"（侍同士が刀で斬り合うこと）ショー。"チャンバラ"の体験コーナーもある。（1日4回、各15分）

シネマスタジオ・ライブ撮影の時間ですよ
Visitors are given a humorous look at how period dramas, jidaigeki, are filmed, right on the actual film sets. (4 times a day, 15 minutes long)
スタジオセットの中で、時代劇撮影の裏側を定番シーンを通して笑いを交えながら再現する。（1日4回、各15分）

Let's SAMURAI experiences   Let's サムライ体験

1 Start the lesson
レッスン

Learn how to hold and draw the katana, how to cut with it and how to return it to the scabbard.
刀の持ち方や抜き方、斬り方、納め方など基本の所作を学ぶ

2 Get Dressed
着付け

Choose the patterned garment you like best. More than a dozen are on hand.
十数種類の衣装から好きな柄を選び着付けてもらう

3 Get back to the lesson
レッスン再開

Practice the moves you learned wearing real samurai clothing.
実際に侍の衣装を着て、習った技を再度練習

NINJA

Buying Samurai and Ninja Merchandise in the park
村内各店で買える侍&忍者グッズ

Full-scale *katana* reproductions
Katana: From 12,000 yen
リアルに再現された
刀は長さもさまざま
刀　1万2000円〜
※1)

Ninja Show

激突！忍者ショー『サスケ』
Come see the legendary ninja hero Sarutobi Suske in this show packed with vibrant ninja action and 3D projection.
(3 times a day, 20 minutes long)
忍者界の伝説的ヒーロー・猿飛佐助が主人公。忍者らしい躍動感みなぎるアクションと3Dマッピングが一体化した忍者ショー。（1日3回、各20分）

Metal replicas of the weapons used by ninjas to attack opponents
Shuriken (throwing stars): From 500 yen
忍者が手に持って敵に投げつける鉄製の武器のレプリカ
手裏剣 500円〜

Ninja Mystery House

からくり忍者屋敷

Make your way around this ninja house through hidden doors and passageways. The ninja staff members provide guests with an explanation about ninjas and the mechanisms in the house beforehand. (500 yen entry)
"隠し扉" や "隠し通路" などさまざまな場所に仕掛けられたからくりを使いながら忍者屋敷を巡ることができる。最初に忍者姿のスタッフから忍者や仕掛けについての解説がある。（有料500円）

Toei Kyoto Studio Park

東映太秦映画村

A theme park based on an Edo period film set, where visitors can walk freely through sets used in film and television, watch shows featuring ninja and samurai, and experience other attractions.

時代劇を体験できるテーマパーク。映画やテレビ撮影のセットを自由に歩くことができ、侍や忍者に関するショーやアトラクションが人気。

Shuriken Dojo

手裏剣道場

Try your hand at throwing *shuriken* at targets. Staff clad in ninja garments teach you how to get started.
(5 throws for 300 yen, 8 for 500 yen)
忍者の武器である手裏剣を的に命中させるゲーム。忍者姿のスタッフが手裏剣の投げ方をレクチャーしてくれる。（有料5枚300円、8枚500円）

☎075-864-7716
📍P70-B3
🚶5 minute walk from Uzumasa Station on the JR line.
¥2,200 yen (plus fees for some attractions)
🕐9:00-17:00 (depends on month)
Unscheduled

❹ Have your photo taken
記念撮影

Get a photo of you in costume and posing like a real samurai.
最後はポーズをキメて記念写真を撮ることができる

Samurai Kembu Theater
サムライ剣舞シアター

Here visitors can watch an hour-long traditional show in which samurai performers wield swords and fans as they dance to Japanese poetry and classical melodies. When the show is over, people can try on some samurai clothing and take a class in genuine kembu, or sword dancing.
漢詩・和歌や古典文学の旋律に合わせて、侍姿の演者が刀や扇を手に舞う1時間の伝統芸能ステージを見た後、侍の衣装に着替えて本格剣舞レッスンを受けることができる。

☎075-751-2033 📍P80-B1 🚶Near Sanjo Station on the Keihan line
¥Show + Lesson – 8,000 yen http://www.samurai-kembu.jp/
🕐Starts at 13:00 Mon. Wed. Fri. and at 17:00 Mon. - Sat Sun

※1) Please note that the import of reproduction weapons is restricted in some countries.　　※1）模造刀は、持ち込み禁止の国もあるのでご注意ください。

⓴ Kyoto International Manga Museum

京都国際マンガミュージアム

The Holy Land of Manga!

✿ 日本マンガの殿堂!

Manga is one of the cultural staples of Japan. The first library and museum in Japan devoted to manga, the Kyoto International Manga Museum opened in 2006 and has 300,000 items in its collection, comprised primarily of domestic manga. In the "Manga Expo" section, you can read translated versions of popular manga as well as comics published in foreign countries.

日本を代表する文化の一つ・マンガ。京都国際マンガミュージアムは、日本初のマンガの図書館・博物館で2006年にオープン。国内のマンガを中心に30万点の資料を収蔵する。「マンガ万博」コーナーでは、人気マンガの翻訳版や海外で出版されたコミックスも読むことができる。

☎ 075-254-7414 📍 P74-C2
🚶 Near Karasuma-oike Station on the Karasuma subway line [¥] 800yen Re-entry is permitted only on the same day
🕙 10:00 – 18:00 (last admission 17:30) Wednesdays (or Thursday when Wednesday is a national holiday)

Walls of Manga

マンガの壁

These are tall shelves of books that cover the walls of the 1st to 3rd floors. Approximately 50,000 manga representing a wide variety of genres are arrayed in individual book form from floor to ceiling for your reading enjoyment.

1階～3階の各フロアに設置された書架、「マンガの壁」。約5万冊もの幅広いジャンルのマンガ単行本が天井高くまでずらりと並べられ、自由に手にとって読むことができる。

1987 1988 1989 1989

Art Object
Hi no Tori (Phoenix)
火の鳥オブジェ

Tezuka Osamu is a manga artist who made important contributions to the development of Japanese manga and anime. *Hi no Tori* is one of the major characters he created. A gigantic representation of this character produced using techniques utilized in Buddhist sculpture hangs in the 2nd-floor atrium.

日本のマンガやアニメの発展に大きく貢献したマンガ家・手塚治虫。「火の鳥」は、彼の代表キャラクターの一つ。2階の吹抜けに展示されている巨大オブジェは、仏像彫刻の技術をもって制作された。

©Tezuka Productions

Manga Studio
マンガ工房

Young manga artists demonstrate how to create manga, allowing you to see how underdrawing, inking-over and other procedures that you normally would not be able to see are done. Open only on Saturdays, Sundays and holidays.

若手マンガ家によるマンガ制作の実演。下描きやペン入れなど、普段なかなか見られない一つひとつの作業工程を見学できる。土・日曜、祝日のみ開催。

Portrait Corner
似顔絵コーナー

You can have an artist draw a standard likeness of you or request to be portrayed as a character in an anime. It costs 1,000yen per person and takes about 20 minutes.

本人に似せて描いてくれる「スタンダードタッチ」か、アニメの登場人物になったような「アニメタッチ」を選ぶことができる。1人1000円。約20分で完成。

Museum Café MM
ミュージアムカフェ えむえむ

Be sure to check out the room with the counter, where real manga artists have drawn illustrations directly on the walls. You can order lunch, light meals and sweets.

スタンドカフェ内の壁に描かれたマンガ家直筆イラストは必見。ランチや軽食、スイーツを販売。

Azuki-bean parfait 500yen
小豆パフェ 500 円

Fried-noodle bread 380yen
やきそばパン 380 円

Museum Shop
ミュージアムショップ

The shop carries items related to popular manga and anime, as well as original museum items only available here.
You can also purchase translated versions of the latest popular titles and the enduring masterpieces.

人気マンガやアニメのグッズのほか、館内限定のオリジナルグッズも。最新の人気作品から不朽の名作の翻訳版のコミックスまで購入できる。

Original postcard 150yen
オリジナルポストカード 150 円

Astro Boy T-shirt 3,024yen
アトム T シャツ 3024 円

45

21 Sounds of Kyoto

|京都の音|

Listening carefully to the sounds of Kyoto

✿ 京都の音に耳を澄ます

The sounds of life and nature have been considered very important in Japan ever since ancient times. Visitors to Kyoto can still experience sounds that are a product of the ingenuity of people in previous eras and here we learn a bit about how they are created.

古来より日本人は、日々の生活の中で耳にする音や、自然が奏でる音を大切にしてきた。京都では今も、先人たちの工夫が凝らされた独特の音色を聴くことができる。その音色の仕組みについても学んでみよう。

How it works 仕組み

Metal fittings and nails called mekasugai are used to secure corridor floorboards. They also make sounds as they rub against each other when people walk on the floorboards.

廊下の板の固定に使われている「目かすがい」という金属の釘穴と釘が、人が廊下を歩く度に擦れ合い音を発する。

mekasugai (Clamp)
目かすがい

Spike hole
釘穴

Spike
釘

Uguisubari
(Nightingale floor)
うぐいす張り廊下

When people walk on these wooden floors, they make a squeaking sound like the chirp of an uguisu (Japanese bush warbler). One theory suggests that they were designed to alert the inhabitants of intruders such as ninja. You can hear this sound at Nijo-jo Castle (above photo.→P32) and other locations in town.

人が床の板の上を歩くと「キュッ、キュッ」とうぐいすの鳴き声に似たきしみ音を出す。忍者などの侵入者を知らせるための装置という説も。二条城（→P32）などで耳にすることができる。

Temple bells 寺院の鐘

Temples have a large hanging bronze bell that they ring to announce the time, and also to announce such things as the beginning of memorial services. One special Japanese custom is that monks strike the temple bells on the last day of the year. At Daigo-ji Temple (→P9) and other temples, tourists can also strike the bell after receiving a ticket that is distributed in advance.

寺院には青銅製の大きな釣り鐘が設置されており、時刻や法要の始まりなどを告げるために用いられる。また日本の行事の一つに大晦日に僧が鐘をつく習慣があり、醍醐寺（→P9）などでは事前に配布される整理券をもらって観光客もつくことができる。

Shishi-odoshi
(Literally, deer scarer)
ししおどし

This device makes a pleasant knock a few times a minute, adding to the overall atmosphere of a Japanese garden. It was originally created to protect crops by scaring animals away, but Shisen-do Temple was the first to incorporate it as a feature of the temple garden.

「コンッ」と数十秒ごとに響く快い音色を出し、日本庭園において雰囲気を演出する音響装置で、詩仙堂が発祥。元々は、動物が田畑を荒らすのを威嚇して防ぐために作られたもの。

How it works 仕組み

Water enters a bamboo tube that is open at one end. After the weight of the water causes the tube to tip over releasing the water, the sound is produced when the tube rebounds and strikes the stone that it was initially resting on.

片方の口が開いた竹筒に水が注がれ、溜まると水をはき出す。その反動で、元の位置に置かれた石を打つ音を発する。

Knock

○ **Shisen-do Temple**
詩仙堂
☎075-781-2954 ♥ P70-D3
🚶 7 minute walk from the Kyoto City Bus Ichijoji-kudari-matsu-cho bus stop ¥500yen
⏱ 9:00-17:00 (last admission 16:45)
📅 May 23 (Anniversary of Ishikawa Jozan's death)

Suikinkutsu (water koto cave)　水琴窟

This ingenious device is a garden fixture that emits a high-pitched resonation. It originally derives from the culture of the tea ceremony and was a drainage system devised to prevent gardens from becoming flooded during crowded tea ceremonies when participants used water from the chozubachi, or wash basin.

「ポロンポロン」と甲高く響くような音色がする。庭の設備の一つで茶道の文化から生まれたもので、お茶会でたくさんの人が手水鉢を使うことによって、庭が水浸しになってしまうのを防ぐために考案された排水装置。

How it works 仕組み

A jar with a small hole in the bottom is buried upside down near the chozubachi. It makes a resonating sound when water drips into it.

手水鉢の近くに、底に小さな穴を開けた甕を伏せて埋め、漏れ入る水を溜める。そこに雫が落ちて反響することで音を発する。

○ **Taizo-in, sub-temple of Myoshin-ji Temple**
妙心寺 退蔵院
☎075-463-2855 ♥ P78-B3
🚶 Near the Kyoto City Bus Myoshin-ji-mae bus stop
¥500yen
⏱ 9:00-17:00
📅 Open year round 7 days a week

47

Sado ｜茶道｜

The traditional Japanese art of the tea ceremony
✿ 日本伝統の茶の儀式

Sado (the Japanese tea ceremony) is not only about drinking tea. This is a series of ceremonial rituals whereby a host treats a guest (or guests) with tea in accordance with prescribed etiquette and with emphasis placed on the spiritual interaction between the participants. The tea ceremony is said to have attained its present form through the efforts of Sen no Rikyu in the 16th century. Beautiful Japanese sweets, tea utensils and tea gardens developed along with sado, contributing greatly to the development of Japanese traditional culture.

茶道とは、ただお茶を飲むだけのことではない。亭主と客人が、作法に則り精神的な交流し、お茶でもてなし、もてなされるという一連の儀式である。16世紀に千利休が大成したといわれ、美しい和菓子や茶道具、茶庭などは茶道とともに発展、日本の伝統文化に大きく貢献した。

What is a chashitsu (teahouse)?
茶室とは

A chashitsu is a room or building where the tea ceremony is held. The host and guests seat themselves Japanese style in a small tatami-mat room that is about 3m² (standard teahouse size) and can seat up to four or five people. The austere interior prevents distraction from the essence of what is taking place around you, with extraneous elements removed to evoke the feeling of wabi through extreme simplicity.

茶事を行う部屋や建物のこと。約3m四方で4～5人の客人を迎えることができる小さな畳の部屋に、亭主と客人が正座する。物事の本質を追求するため、あらゆる飾り気を排し、簡素でわびを感じるしつらえになっている。

Host 亭主

The person who treats guests to tea. He or she decides the theme of the ceremony and goes to great lengths to please the guests through his or her selection of everything from the tea bowls and utensils to the hanging scroll.
お茶でもてなしをする人。亭主が茶会のテーマを決め、茶碗、道具、掛け軸に至るまで客人のために趣向を凝らしもてなす

Ro (Hearth) 炉

An open hearth that is used in winter to boil water in a chagama(kettle).
冬の季節に茶釜の湯を沸かすための囲炉裏

Guests 客人

Those who are treated tea.
お茶でもてなしを受ける人

Kakejiku (Hanging scroll) 掛け軸

Hung at the tokonoma, the calligraphy or other items represents the theme of the tea ceremony.
床の間に掛ける、茶席のテーマを表す書など

Flowers お花

Seasonal flowers are used as decoration and are one element of the hospitality accorded to the guests.
季節の花を飾る。客人へのもてなしの一つ

Tokonoma (Alcove) 床の間

Tokonoma are found in Japanese-style guest rooms and serve as a place to hang scrolls or locate arranged flowers and other decorative items.
和室の客間にある小さな空間で、掛け軸や生け花などを飾るところ

Utensils used for Sado 茶道具

Chasen 茶筅

A bamboo utensil used for mixing together the matcha and hot water in a tea bowl.
茶碗に入れた抹茶と湯を混ぜる道具。竹製。

Natsume 棗

A container used to hold matcha. They are generally lacquerware.
抹茶を入れる容器。漆塗りのものが一般的。

Chashaku (Tea scoop) 茶杓

A scoop used specifically for matcha green-tea powder.
抹茶をすくうさじ。

Chagama (Kettle) 茶釜

A pot used for boiling water to make tea.
お茶をたてるための湯を沸かす釜。

Hishaku (Ladle) 柄杓

A bamboo utensil used for scooping up both hot and cold water.
お湯や水をすくう道具。竹製。

General flow of the tea ceremony お茶をいただく流れ

1 Purify your hands and mouth
手と口を清める

Wash and purify your hands and mouth with water from the *tsukubai*, a rock

basin set outside the teahouse.
茶室の外にある水の入った石・つくばいの水で口と手を洗い身を清める。

2 Enter the teahouse
茶室に入る

Kneeling with your head tilted forward, enter from the nijiriguchi entrance. This posture is a gesture of respect for the space prepared by the host, and indicates equality among the guests.

にじり口より身を屈めながら、正座姿で入る。亭主が作り上げた空間に敬意を払い客人同士が平等であるという意味がある。

3 Seat yourself
席に着く

Once seated, you can appreciate the hanging scroll and flowers, as well as the host's otemae (the way in which the tea is made).
席に着いたら、掛け軸と花を観賞し、お点前(お茶を点てる美しい所作)を拝見する。

4 Eat the confectionery
和菓子を食べる

Seasonal Japanese sweets are provided as they enhance the flavor of the tea. Eat them while holding the *kaishi* paper.
日本の四季を表す和菓子はお茶を引き立てるために出されるもの。懐紙を手に持って食べる。

5 Enjoy your tea
茶をいただく

The host presents you with the tea bowl with the most beautiful part facing you. You gently rotate the tea bowl clockwise twice to subtly avoid the front, and enjoy the tea in several

sips rather than all at once.
亭主が茶碗の最も美しい部分を正面として差し出す。茶碗を2度回し正面を少し外したところが飲み口で、数回に分けお茶を味わって飲む。

6 How to finish drinking
飲み終わりのマナー

It is polite to make a quick sipping noise as you have the last sip to express that the tea was great. Use your thumb and forefinger to wipe off the edge of the bowl where you had placed

your lips, and rotate it twice in the reverse direction to bring the front back to you.
飲み終わるときに吸い込むように「スッ」という音を立て、おいしかったという意味を表すことが礼儀。口を付けた縁を親指と人差し指でぬぐい、茶碗を元の位置に戻す。

7 Appreciate the tea bowl and utensils
茶碗や道具を拝見

Hold the tea bowl, and then other utensils, to appreciate the shape and colors and other aspects of the design.

お茶碗などを両手で持ちながら茶碗の色・形などを楽しむ。

Sen no Rikyu
千利休 (1522 ～ 1591)

The founder of the *Senke* school of tea ceremony. Under his direction, the tea ceremony developed so as to occupy part of the artistic culture, culminating in "*wabicha*" (the tea ceremony as characterized by rustic simplicity). Rikyu worked in the service of Toyotomi Hideyoshi, the most powerful political figure of the day, but incurred his wrath and was forced to commit seppuku, or hara-kiri.

千家流茶道の祖。茶道を芸術性に富んだ文化に発展させ、「侘茶」を大成した。時の権力者・豊臣秀吉に仕えたが、彼の怒りにふれ、切腹した。

Places where you can do sado (chado) in English 英語対応の茶道体験施設

Kyoto Washinkan 京都和心館
WAK-WAK-KAN わくわく館

Visit these two facilities run by WAK JAPAN where you can experience traditional Japanese culture. Located near Sanjusangen-do Temple. Washinkan has incorporated aspects of "universal design," while Wakuwaku-kan makes use of a 100-year-old *machiya* townhouse located near Kyoto Imperial Palace.

ワックジャパンが運営する日本の伝統文化を体験できる二施設。三十三間堂の近くにある和心館はユニバーサルデザインを施し、築約100年の歴史ある町家を利用したわくわく館は京都御所の近くにある。

☎075-212-9993(WAK JAPAN)
📍P73-E2(kyoto Washinkan) 📍P75-D1(WAK-WAK-KAN)
🚶 [¥] 🕐 💳 http://www.wakjapan.com

ran Hotei
らん布袋

Run by a Canadian master of the way of tea, there is also a café where you can casually enjoy drinking matcha and having matcha sweets.

カナダ人の茶道家がオーナー。抹茶や抹茶スイーツを気軽に楽しめるカフェも併設。

☎075-801-0790 📍P74-B2
🚶15 minute walk from Nijo Station on the JR line
[¥] 3,500yen 🕐 11:30 – 20:00 from Monday to Wednesday, 11:30 – 23:00 on Fridays, and 11:00 – 20:00 on Saturdays and Sundays 💳 Thursdays

Maiko | 舞妓 |

Go to see maiko!

☆ 舞妓さんに会いに行こう!

Maiko and geiko are female performers who perform music and dance on a stage or at a banquet. Maiko are apprentices usually between 15 and 20 years old who become geiko when they finish their trainning. In Kyoto, there are five *kagai* (*geisha* districts). They live in an *okiya* (teahouse which maiko and geiko belong to) to learn traditional customs and performances.

舞妓・芸妓とは舞台や宴会で音楽や踊りといった伝統芸能を披露する女性パフォーマーのこと。15～20歳くらいまでの修行中は舞妓、成長すると芸妓になる。京都には花街が5つあり、舞妓・芸妓は置屋（所属する家）に住み込み、伝統的なしきたりや芸を学ぶ。

1 *Gion Corner* is a facility where you can see seven kinds of traditional performance. *Kyo-mai* (Kyoto-style dance) performed by *maiko* is a must-see. ☎ 075-561-1119 ♥P80-B3 [¥] 3,150yen
1. ギオンコーナーは、7つの伝統芸能を鑑賞できる施設。舞妓の京舞は必見

2 *On Shiraka-wa-minami-dori Street* late in the afternoon, you may come across *maiko* heading to a banquet. ♥P80-A2
2. 白川南通では夕方、お座敷に向かう舞妓にすれ違うことも

3 *Around Hanami-ko-ji-dori Street*, there are many *okiya*, as well as banquet places and high-class restaurants where guests are entertained by *maiko* and *geiko*. ♥P80-B3
3. 花見小路通界隈は置屋や、舞妓・芸妓がお客さんを接待するお座敷・お茶屋が数多く立ち並ぶ

4 *Tatsumi-daimyojin Shrine* is a shrine that *maiko* visit to pray for improving the technique of their arts. ♥P80-B2
4. 芸事上達を願って舞妓さんがおまいりする辰巳大明神

5 *You are served by maiko at Miyagawa-cho Beer Garden.* It's open from mid-July to late August(tentative) ☎ 075-561-1151 Miyaga-wa-cho Ochaya Association. ♥P80-A3 [¥] 5,000yen
5. 宮川町ビアガーデンでは舞妓さんが接客してくれる。期間は7月中旬～8月下旬（予定）

The Maiko style
舞妓さん

Makeup 化粧

Maiko have their face painted white (by applying *oshiroi* face powder), and eyebrows and eyes with two colors of red and black. For their lips, those who are in the 1st year of apprenticeship have only their lower lip painted red.

顔は均一に白く塗り（おしろい）、眉と目は赤と黒の2色で化粧。1年目の舞妓は下唇だけ口紅をさす。

Obi sash 帯

The *darari-obi* is a type of belt that hangs at the back and is a feature of *maiko* clothing. They are custommade and contain gold and silver threads, which makes them very expensive. They can be as much as 5 to 6 meters long and are quite heavy.

舞妓の象徴、背中の下に長く垂らす「だらりの帯」は特注品で、金糸、銀糸が使われ非常に高価。長さ5〜6mもあり重い。

Hair 髪

Their hair is parted into four sections in a style called *ware-shinobu*. The ornamental hairpins worn change with the changing flowers and events of each season.

地毛を4ブロックに分けたヘアスタイル「割れしのぶ」。月替わりで季節の花や行事にちなんだ「かんざし」を挿す。

Okobo おこぼ

Okobo are shoes that can be up to 10cm high. Those worn by novice *maiko* have a bell inside that makes a sound every time they walk.

高さが10cmもある履物。新米の舞妓のおこぼには内側に鈴が付けられ、歩くたびに音が鳴る。

*Please respect the personal space of the *maiko* and *geiko* by not asking to have photos taken with them. They are not mascots of the city, but individuals engaged in employment.
※舞妓・芸妓さんにむやみに撮影を依頼してはいけません。京都のマスコットではなく仕事中です。

Be transformed into a maiko! 舞妓に変身!

Completion

Maiko Transformation Studio Shiki
舞妓変身スタジオ 四季

After being made up in exactly the same makeup and clothing as *maiko*, you can go out and about and get photos taken.
舞妓と全く同じように化粧と着付けをし、その姿で外出や写真撮影ができる。

☎075-531-2777
📍P80-C4
🚶6 minute walk from the Kyoto City Bus Kiyomizu-michi bus stop
💴Maiko Studio Plan: from 14,040yen, Sansaku (Walkabout) Plan: from 18,630yen
🕘9:00 – last admission 17:00 (last admission 15:00 for plans with outdoor photo-shooting or walkabout)
📅Open year round 7 days a week

1　Apply *oshiroi* (white face powder) to your neck and face, and rouge to your eyes and lips.
首と顔に「おしろい」を塗り、目元、口元に紅をさす。

2　Apply a *maiko* hairpiece, blending it in with your own hair, and put on *kanzashi*.
舞妓のカツラを地毛になじませてかぶり、かんざしも付ける。

3　Choose a *kimono* you like from a variety of colors and patterns, and have it put on you.
豊富な色柄から好きな着物を選び着付けてもらえる。

㉔ Kyo-machiya

| 京町家 |

Traditional Kyoto architecture

✿ 伝統的な京都の建築

Kyo-machiya are a traditional form of residence with a long tradition in Kyoto, with many homes built side-by-side facing the street, often sharing a roof, and providing both living and working space. They are often referred to as "eel beds" because the frontage is narrow with the house itself stretching far back from the street. Their beauty and functionality have led many people in recent years to repurpose them in a variety of ways, including as restaurants and hotels.

京町家は古くから京都に伝わる伝統的な住まいで、通りに面して隣の家と軒を連ねて立つ。店と住居を兼ねている場合もある。間口が狭く奥に長いことから「うなぎの寝床」と呼ばれる。美しさと機能性を兼ね備えた町家は、近年飲食店や宿泊施設などに再利用され人気を集めている。

Mushikomado windows
虫籠窓

Often found in *machiya* with a low-roofed second story facade, these windows allow light in and provide ventilation.
2階の天井が低く中二階となる作りの町家に多くみられる。採光、通風の効果がある

Statue of Zhong Kui
鍾馗さん

Tile statues such as this stand on roofs to ward off evil and protect the house.
屋根の上に立つ瓦製の像。家を守る魔よけの神様とされる

Lattice windows
格子窓

These windows are designed such that the interior is not very visible from the bright outdoors, while people on the dark inside can see out with ease.
明るい外から見えにくく、暗い中からはよく見える構造の窓

Yamanaka Aburaten Machiya Guest House
http://www.yoil.co.jp/mghouse/en/
山中油店 町家ゲストハウス

Kyo-machiya restaurants and other establishments 京町家を利用した施設

🏠 Tondaya - Nishijin Lifestyle Museum
西陣くらしの美術館 冨田屋

At this approximately 130-year-old townhouse, you can view the architecture, experience Japanese culture, and learn about traditional Kyoto customs.
築約130年の町家で、建物の見学や文化体験、京都のしきたりが学べる。

☎075-432-6701 📍P76-B3
🚶5 minute walk from the Kyoto City Bus Ichijo-modoribashi or Seimei-jinja-mae bus stop ¥2,160yen~ (reservation required)
🕙10:00 – 18:00 📅Open year round 7 days a week

✖ Daikokuden Honpo Seien
大極殿本舗 栖園

This traditional Japanese sweet shop was established in 1885. One popular confection they are known for is Kohaku-nagashi (660yen), made of high-quality agar-agar topped with molasses.
1885年創業の老舗の甘味処。上質な寒天に白蜜がかかる琥珀流し 660円が名物。

☎075-221-3311 📍P75-D1
🚶7 minute walk from Shijo Station on the Karasuma subway line
🕙10:00 – last call 17:00 📅Wednesdays

Inside machiya
京町家の内観

Okudo-san　おくどさん

This term is used only in Kyoto and refers to the cooking furnace, or kamado.

京都特有の呼び名で竈のこと。

Tokonoma　床の間

Tokonoma are found in guest rooms and serve as a place to hang scrolls or locate other decorative items.

客間にあり、掛け軸などを飾る場所。

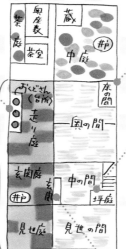

Tsuboniwa　坪庭

The courtyard garden is both esthetically pleasing and functional in that it provides light and ventilation.

家屋内に設けられた採光と風通し効果を得るための小さな庭で鑑賞用。

Toriniwa　通り庭

This dirt-floored passageway stretches from the entrance all the way to the backyard and has a vaulted ceiling that allows heat to escape.

熱を逃がすよう吹き抜けになった土間で、入口から裏庭まで続く。

Genkan　玄関

This area serves to divide the commercial-use space from the residential space.

商業用と住居用のスペースを区切る役割。

🛒 Yamanaka Cooking Oil
山中油店

This shop was established around 200 years ago and specializes in culinary and edible oils. Tamajime-shibori Sesame Oil has a rich sesame flavor and is available for 1,188yen(450g). Their olive oil products are also popular.

創業約200年の食用油専門店。ゴマの風味豊かな玉締めしぼり胡麻油は1188円(450g)。オリーブオイルも評判。

☎075-841-8537 📍P76-B4
🚶3 minute walk from the Kyoto City Bus Marutamachi-chiekoin bus stop ⏱8:30 – 17:00 ⊘Sundays and holidays

🍴 AWOMB
AWOMB

This restaurant provides you with dried sheets of seaweed onto which you place vinegared rice, fresh gluten cakes, vegetables, spices and other ingredients to make your own sushi rolls. Teori Sushi: from 1,680yen.

海苔の上に酢飯を乗せ、生麩や野菜やスパイスなどを巻き込み食べる手巻き寿司スタイルのメニュー。手織り寿し(並)1680円〜。

☎075-204-5543 📍P74-C2
🚶6 minute walk from Shijo Station on the karasuma subway line ⏱12:00 – 15:00, 18:00 – 20:00 ⊘Unscheduled

Nishiki-ichiba Market

錦市場

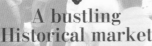

A bustling Historical market

☙ 歴史ある市場

This market is a 390 m long street lined with around 130 shops that has operated for roughly 400 years. It is known as "Kyoto's kitchen" because you can find foodstuffs from Kyoto and all around Japan as well as high-quality cooking equipment. The market bustles with locals and tourists every day.

約 400 年の歴史を誇る錦市場は、390 m にわたって約 130 の店が道の両側に軒を連ねる。京都をはじめ日本全国の食材や高品質の調理器具が揃うことから「京の台所」とも呼ばれ、地元の人や観光客で連日賑わう。

- 📍 P75-D3 🚶 4 minute walk from Shijo Station on the Karasuma subway line / 4 minute walk from Kawaramachi Station on the Hankyu line

2 Konnamonja
こんなもんじゃ

This shop is owned and managed by Kyo-tofu Fujino, a famous *tofu* shop. They sell freshly deep-fried soy milk doughnuts made from soymilk. They are not too sweet and the airy texture is addicting.

豆腐の有名店・京とうふ藤野の直営店。豆乳を使った豆乳ドーナツは揚げたてを販売。甘さ控えめで、ふわふわの食感がたまらない。

Soy milk doughnuts : 300yen/10 doughnuts
豆乳ドーナツ 10 個入り 300 円

- ☎ 075-255-3231 📍 P75-D3
- 🕙 10:00 – 18:00 📅 Open year round 7 days a week

Takakura-dori Street

Sakaimachi-dori Street

Yanaginobanba-dori Street

Chopstick rest :
From 540yen
箸置き 1 個 540 円~

Chopsticks :
From 860yen/pair
箸 1 膳 860 円~

1 Kitchen Yuzen
きっちん遊膳

This shop carries approximately 800 kinds of chopsticks, on some of which you can have your name engraved for free. Many of the chopstick rests feature unique design motifs.

約 800 種類の箸を取り揃える。箸に無料で名前を彫刻してもらえる商品もある。箸置きはユニークなモチーフが多い。

- ☎ 075-212-3390 📍 P75-D3 🕙 10:00-18:00
- 📅 Open year round 7 days a week

1. Kizami-suguki (Chopped pickled suguki turnip) : 432yen *2. Shibazuke (Chopped salted vegetables with red perilla)* : 464yen
1. きざみすぐき 432 円 2. しば漬 464 円

3 Uchida Tsukemono
 打田漬物

Shibazuke, one of the most popular kinds of pickles in Japan, and *suguki-zuke*, more particular to Kyoto, are just part of the variety of pickles this shop carries, which includes Chinese yams and other vegetables not usually used for pickling. You can taste most items before making a purchase.

日本定番のしば漬や京都定番のすぐき漬け、漬物には珍しい野菜・長いもの漬物もある。この店では、ほとんどの商品を試食してから購入できる。

- ☎ 075-221-5609 📍 P75-D3
- 🕙 9:00 – 18:00 📅 Open year round 7 days a week

Nagaimo-wasabi (Chinese yam flavored with wasabi) : 540yen
長いも わさび 540 円

4 Kuromame Saan Kitao
黒豆茶庵 北尾

This bean specialty shop sells a select variety of beans, including the highest-class black beans from Kyoto, as well as bean products. Popular among them are sweets with the rich flavor of black beans.

京都産の最高級黒豆をはじめ厳選された豆や、豆製品が並ぶ専門店。黒豆の風味豊かなスイーツ類が人気。

☎075-212-0088
📍P75-D3
🕘9:30 – 18:00
(Café: 11:00 - 17:30)
📅Wednesdays
*Subject to change according to the season

Toasted-black-bean-flour soft ice cream :
Take-out:324yen,
Eat-in:486yen

黒豆きなこ
ソフトクリーム
テイクアウト 324 円
イートイン 486 円

Poripori, a snack sprinkled with toasted-bean flour :
394yen
きな粉をまぶしたスナック菓子
ぽりぽり 394 円

Tominokoji-dori Street		Fuyacho-dori Street		Gokomachi-dori Street	Teramachi-dori Street	Shinkyogoku-dori Street

4　5　6

Nishikikoji-dori Street

Nishiki tenman-gu Shrine
錦天満宮

Kyo Machiya Nishiki Agaru
京町家 錦上ル

You can bring food items that you purchased in the market here to eat. Each person in your group must, however, order at least one drink, rice dish, desert or other item for 540yen from the menu.
市場で購入したお総菜などの食品を持ち込んで食べられる食事処。ドリンク、ごはん、デザートなどから1人何か1品540円のオーダーが必要。

☎075-257-7666　📍P75-D2
🕘(Eat-in café) 11:00 – last call 16:00　📅Mondays

---

6 Aritsugu
有次

Aritsugu is a well-established cooking utensil shop with a history of more than 450 years. Their fans include many professionals who come to buy knives, pots, graters and other cooking utensils carefully made using traditional methods.

創業約450年を超える料理道具の名店。伝統的な手法によって丁寧に作られる包丁や鍋、卸し金などの調理器具はプロの愛用者も多い。

☎075-221-1091　📍P75-D3
🕘9:00-17:30　📅Open year round 7 days a week

Cooking mold :
From 1,080yen
抜き型　1080 円〜

Santoku general purposes knife
: 16,740yen
三徳包丁　1万6740 円

---

5 Cha, Yamadashiya
茶・やまだしや

This shop sells a wide variety of Japanese tea leaves. The savory aroma of freshly roasted tea leaves wafts through the air at the shopfront where you can specify by weight the amount of tea you wish to purchase.

種類豊富な日本茶が揃う店。茶葉を煎る芳ばしい香りがする店頭では、煎りたての新鮮な茶葉を必要な分だけ計量して購入できる。

Tea leaves: : From 648yen/100g
お茶　648 円 /100g 〜
☎075-223-5272　📍P75-D3
🕘10:00 – 18:00　📅Wednesdays

26) Gifts from Japan
| 和みやげ |

Items made using traditional techniques
✿ 伝統の技を感じるアイテム

Some of the most popular souvenirs and gifts include craftworks from the older Kyoto shops and modern items using traditional techniques.

京都の老舗店が手掛ける工芸品や、伝統技法を現代風にアレンジしたグッズは、おみやげや贈り物にも大人気。

Gifts

Furoshiki
風呂敷

Large cotton furoshiki: 5,616yen each
大判木綿風呂敷各 5616 円

Furoshiki is an approximately 1m-square cloth used to wrap and carry things. You can tie the ends together so that it functions as a bag able to carry about 10kg, or even use it as wall decoration.
品物を包み持ち運ぶための約1m四方の布。端を結べばバッグにもなり、重さ10kgほどの耐久性がある。壁掛けにもなる。

○ Kyoto Kakefuda 京都 掛札
☎075-821-3230 ♥P80-B2
🚶 5 minute walk from Higashiyama Station on the Tozai subway line
🕙 10:00 – 18:00 🚫 Tuesdays (open when Tuesday is a national holiday)

Gamaguchi saifu ※
がま口財布

※ Metal-clasp coin purse

Unlock the metal clasp to allow this purse to open wide and make it easy to remove coins. All of the products in this shop are handmade by professional craftspeople and they come in a variety of sizes, colors and patterns.
金属製の留め具をはずすと大きく口が開き小銭が取り出しやすい。この店の商品は全て職人の手作りでサイズや色柄も豊富。

○ Matsuhiro Shoten
まつひろ商店
☎075-761-5469 ♥P80-B1
🚶 5 minute walk from Higashiyama Station on the Tozai subway line 🕙 10:30 – 20:00
🚫 Open year round 7 days a week

Maru 2.6-sun (about 7.8cm): 735yen each
丸 2.6 寸（約 7.8cm) 各 735 円

Tabi socks
足袋

Tabishita (tabi socks): 540yen/pair
足袋下 1 足 540 円

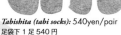

Haritsuke jikatabi (Jikatabi with glued soles): 8,424yen
貼付地下足袋 8424 円

Tabi are traditional Japanese socks that are split into two at the toes. *Jikatabi* which are rubber-soled tabi traditionally worn by Japanese carpenters, are now a stylish part of modern footwear.
指先が 2 つに分かれた日本古来の靴下。足袋の底にゴムを貼った地下足袋は本来日本の大工靴だが、現代風にアレンジしてオシャレに。

SOU・SOU Tabi ○
SOU・SOU 足袋
☎075-212-8005 ♥P75-D3
🚶 5 minute walk from Kawaramachi Station on the Hankyu line
🕙 11:00 – 20:00 🚫 Open year round 7 days a week

Gauze tenugui:
1,728yen each
ガーゼ手ぬぐい
各 1728 円

Aburatori-gami*

※ Oil-blotting facial paper

あぶらとり紙

These remarkably thin pieces of Japanese paper are perfect for blotting away facial oil. This product line popular since 1920 has a logo featuring the face of a woman from Kyoto reflected in a hand-mirror.
顔の皮脂を抑えるのにベストなとても薄い和紙。手鏡に映る京女のロゴがモチーフの看板商品は 1920 年頃から続く人気商品。

Aburatori-gami (20 pieces): 356yen
あぶらとり紙（20枚入り）356 円

Yojiya Sanjo Store Shop&Cafe ○
よーじや 三条店 ショップ＆カフェ
☎075-221-4501 ♀P75-D2
🚶5 minute walk from Kyoto-shiyakusyo-mae Station on the Tozai subway line
🕐11:00 – 19:00
📅Open year round 7 days a week

Tenugui*

手ぬぐい

※ Washcloth

Tenugui are thin cotton washcloths that have been used in Japan for many centuries. They often sport fashionable designs, so are used not only as handkerchiefs, but also as scarves and wall-hangings.
日本で昔から使われる薄い木綿製のタオル。ハンカチ代わりだけでなく、ファッショナブルな色柄もあるので、マフラーやタペストリーにもなる。

○ RAAK
RAAK
☎075-222-8870 ♀P74-C2
🚶3 minute walk from Karasuma Oike Station on the Karasuma subway line 🕐11:00 – 19:00
📅Open year round 7 days a week

Sensu are folding fans made using Japanese paper. This sensu specialty shop was established in 1826 and sells fans painted with elegant seasonal motifs. Some items have been designed to be used as room decoration.
和紙でできた携帯用の扇。1826 年創業のこの扇子専門店では、四季折々の優雅な絵柄が描かれた扇を扱う。インテリア用もある。

Sensu*

※ Folding fan

扇子

Miyawaki Baisen-an ○
宮脇賣扇庵
☎075-221-0181 ♀P75-D2
🚶7 minute walk from Karasuma Oike Station on the Karasuma subway line
🕐9:00 – 18:00 (until 19:00 in summer)
📅Open year round 7 days a week

Ornamental sensu, Shin-botan:
8,640yen
飾り扇 新ぼたん 8640 円
Black sensu stand: 3,240yen
黒塗り台 3240 円

Geta sandals

下駄

Geta are wooden sandals. They are usually worn with traditional Japanese dress, but go well with jeans and a T-shirt as well. The artisans at this shop will adjust the hanao (the cloth thong that holds your foot on the base) for a more comfortable fit.
木製の日本のサンダル。主に和装のときに履くがジーンズやTシャツとも相性抜群。職人が足に合うよう鼻緒（台と足を留める紐）を調整する。

○ Choboya
ーや（ちょぼや）
☎075-561-5584 ♀P80-B2
🚶3 minute walk from Gion Shijo Station on the Keihan line 🕐12:00 – 21:00
📅Sundays and holidays

Ryoba, shiraki (plain wood): 15,000yen
両歯（りょうば）白木 1 万 5000 円

Postcards

はがき

Postcard: 324yen each
はがき各 324 円

These postcards are very tasteful, being hand-made on Japanese paper using traditional woodblock printing techniques. There are about 30 different designs to choose from.
この店のはがきは、伝統的な木版画の技術で職人が和紙に手摺りしており、味わいがある。約 30 種類を販売。

Takezasa-do ○
竹笹堂
☎075-353-8585 ♀P74-C3
🚶8 minute walk from Karasuma Shijo Station on the Karasuma subway line 🕐11:00 – 18:00 (from 13:00 in winter)
📅Sundays and holidays

Japanese confectionery

| 和菓子 |

Delicious works of art

✿ 美味しいアート作品

Many Japanese sweets are made with sweet red bean simmered in sugared water, and they tend to have fewer calories than Western sweets. Sweets in Kyoto evolved alongside the tea ceremony, and many are used to artistically express different aspects of the seasons in subtle colors and shapes.

和菓子には小豆を砂糖で炊いた餡を使ったものが多く、洋菓子よりも低カロリー。京都の和菓子は茶道とともに発展した。日本の四季の風物を巧みに表現したものも多く、美しく繊細な色や形をした芸術品だ。

和菓子の12か月

Sweets of the month

1月 / January

Daffodil
水仙
Expresses the early arrival of spring
一足早い春の訪れを表現

2月 / February

Camellia hiemalis
寒椿
A type of camellia that blooms in the depths of winter.
寒中に花開く椿

3月 / March

Butterfly
胡蝶
Butterfly dancing in a spring field
春の野を舞う蝶

4月 / April

Warming of water
みず温む
Expressed as the glistening and wavering surface of a pond
池の水面が輝き揺れるさま

5月 / May

Green leaves
青葉
In the shape of new green leaves
新緑の若葉をかたどったもの

6月 / June

Young sweetfish
若鮎
In the form of sweetfish energetically swimming in a river
川を泳ぐ、元気のよい鮎の姿

Water trickling from rocks
岩清水
Expresses water welling up from between stones
岩の間から湧き出る水を表現

7月 / July

8月 / August

Summer appearance
夏姿
The dangling sleeve of a *yukata* kimono
浴衣の袖が揺れるさま

9月 / September

Moon-viewing rabbit
月見うさぎ
Image of a rabbit hopping about on a moonlit night
月夜に跳ねるウサギの姿

Depicts the gradations of color seen in autumn leaves
モミジのグラデーション

Kyo-arashiyama
京嵐山

10月 / October

11月 / November

Kyo-kabura turnip
京かぶら
Traditional Kyoto produce said to bring good luck
京の冬野菜・かぶらは縁起物

12月 / December

White plum flower
白梅
Symbolizes the coming new year
待ち遠しい新春を表す

Learn about Japanese confectionery 和菓子について学ぼう

Kyoto Confectionery Museum (Kyo-gashi Shiryokan) was founded by the long-running Kyoto sweet shop Tawaraya Yoshitomi. Here you can learn the history of Kyoto confectionery, and enjoy some tea and sweets in the tea room (700 yen).

京菓子の老舗・俵屋吉富が設立した京菓子資料館。京菓子の歴史を学び、併設のお茶室でお茶と和菓子を食べることができる(700円)。

Kyo-gashi Shiryokan○
京菓子資料館
☎075-432-3101 (Tawaraya Yoshitomi, Karasuma Shop) ♥P76-C2
🚶5 minute walk from Imadegawa Station on the Karasuma subway line
￥Free ⏰10:00-17:00 ⊗Wednesdays

There are wooden confectionery molds on display, as well as panels showing the processes of making Japanese sweets.
木製の菓子型や和菓子作りの工程をパネルで展示

Make your own sweets! 和菓子作り体験をしよう!

Kanshun-do is a confectionery shop founded in 1865, and at their Higashi shop, visitors can learn how to make their own authentic Japanese sweets from a professional confectioner.

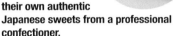

1865年創業の和菓子店・甘春堂 東店では職人の指導を受けながら本格的な和菓子作り体験ができる。

○*Kanshun-do, Higashi shop*
甘春堂 東店
☎075-561-1318 ♥P73-E1
🚶10 minute walk from Shichijo Station on the Keihan line ⏰9:00-18:00 (Tearoom 10:00-17:00)
ℹ Open year round 7 days a week
Workshop
￥2,160yen (Three unbaked sweets and one dry sweet)
⏰day 9:15-/ 11:00-/ 13:00-/ 15:00-
⏱Time required: About 75 minutes
Things to bring: N/A
Reservation: Required

① Listen to the explanation about the sweets you wish to make
作るお菓子の説明をきく

From their monthly seasonal selection, receive instruction for the three kinds of unbaked sweets and one kind of dry sweet (unbaked item shown in photo). ※
季節(1か月毎)で変わる生菓子3種類と干菓子1種類の説明を受ける

② Learn about the tools
道具の説明をきく
You will learn about the tools of the trade, including the "triangular wood pallet", used to shape sweets, and mold.
成形に使う「三角ヘラ」「抜き型」などの道具類の説明を受ける

③ Make sweets under the guidance of a confectioner
職人の指導のもと作る

As the ingredients are soft and small, you must pay careful attention to the angle of your fingertips and how much pressure you apply when shaping the sweets.
素材が柔らかく小さいので、指先の力加減や角度に気を配りながら成形する

④ Eat the completed sweets
完成したお菓子をいただく

You can eat the completed sweets with some *matcha* green tea. Dry sweets are better for taking home.
完成した和菓子をお抹茶と一緒に試食できる。干菓子は持ち帰りがおすすめ

※Dry sweets (higashi) is a dry kind of Japanese confection that contains almost no moisture. ※干菓子とは、ほぼ水分を含まない乾燥した和菓子のこと

28

Matcha Sweets

| 抹茶スイーツ |

Bitter and sweet never tasted so good together!

✿ ほのかな苦みと甘さが絶妙！

The Uji area of Kyoto has long been a famous production center of green tea. Powdered green tea is called matcha. In Kyoto, matcha is used in various foods, especially in a wide variety of popular sweets. Many of them keep for a long time, making them great gift ideas as well.

京都・宇治は古来より有数の緑茶の産地として知られる。その緑茶を粉末にしたものが抹茶。京都では多様な食品に抹茶が使われ、特にスイーツはバリエーションも豊富で人気だ。日持ちするものも多いのでおみやげにも最適。

Parfait
パフェ

Tokusen Tsujiri Parfait

特選都路里パフェ *1,383yen*

Be ready to wait in line at this café famous for its *matcha* parfaits. There's all the matcha you could want, from the ice cream to toppings that include *matcha*-flavored castella sponge cake, jelly and whipped cream.

抹茶パフェの有名店で行列必至。抹茶味のカステラ、ゼリー、ホイップクリーム、アイスなど抹茶尽くしの逸品。

Saryo Tsujiri ○
茶寮都路里

☎075-561-2257 ♀P80-B2
🚶3 minute walk from Gion Shijo Station on the Keihan line
🕐10:00-last call 21:00 (last call 20:30 on Saturdays, Sundays and holidays)
📅Open year round 7 days a week

Toji Komeko Waffle, Matcha

東寺米粉ワッフル 抹茶 *200yen*

This waffle is made using rice flour and a generous amount of aromatic matcha. It's not too sweet and has a moist and firm texture. There is only a limited number available each day because they are made by hand.

米粉と香り高い抹茶をふんだんに使った、甘さ控えめでしっとりもちもちのワッフル。手作りのため数量限定。

Bracken-starchdumplings (Warabi-mochi) わらびもち

Matcha warabi-mochi

抹茶わらび餅 *778yen*

Warabi-mochi are particularly soft, pleasantly bitter dumplings with matcha kneaded into the dough. Enjoy with some dark molasses and a sprinkling of toasted soy bean flour mixed with more matcha.

抹茶が練り込まれたわらびもちは、独特の柔らかさで、すっきりとした渋みが特徴。黒蜜と抹茶きな粉をかけて食べる。

○Kyo Hayashiya
京はやしや

☎075-231-3198 ♀P80-A1
🚶2 minute walk from Sanjo Station on the Keihan line
🕐11:30-last call 21:00
📅Open year round 7 days a week

Waffle
ワッフル

Toji Temple ○
(Gift shop on the temple grounds)
東寺（境内売店）

☎075-691-3325 ♀P72-B3
🚶10 minute walk from Toji Station on the Kintetsu line
🕐8:30-16:30 (-17:30 from Mar. 20 to Sep.19)
📅Open year round 7 days a week

Smoothie
スムージー

Kyo-Latte Smoothie Yatsuhashi

京ラテ スムージー 八つ橋

Ⓢ*594yen*, Ⓛ*648yen*

Bittersweet Matcha smoothie with a crushed *Yatsuhashi* cracker for a crispy texture. It is topped by sweet red-bean paste, whipped cream and soft unbaked *Yatsuhashi*.
ほろ苦い抹茶スムージーにカリカリ食感のクラッシュ八つ橋が入る。餡とクリーム、八つ橋をトッピング。

Ⓞ *Tsujiri* 辻利
☎075-551-0220 ♀P80-A2
🚶1 minute walk from Gion Shijo Station on the Keihan line
🕚11:00-20:00 💬Open year round 7 days a week

Cookie
クッキー

Cha-no Ka (10 cookies)

茶の菓 10枚入り   *1,360yen*

Two langue de chat cookies with the robust flavor of matcha and a slice of white chocolate sandwiched in between create a superb balance of bitter and sweet. Sold exclusively in Kyoto.
濃茶生地のラングドシャでホワイトチョコレートをサンド。苦味と甘味が絶妙にマッチする。京都限定商品。

Ⓞ *Kyoto Kitayama Malebranche, Kiyomizu-zaka shop*
京都北山マールブランシュ 清水坂店
☎075-551-5885 ♀P80-C4
🚶6 minute walk from the Kyoto City Bus Kiyomizu-michi bus stop
🕘9:00-18:00
💬Open year round 7 days a week

Baumkuchen
バームクーヘン

Premium Kyo Baum, Enryoku

プレミアム京ばあむ 圓緑   *1,944yen*

This fluffy baumkuchen is made using mild soy milk produced in Kyoto and supreme fragrant matcha from Uji. It is sold exclusively at the Hanami-koji Shop.
京都産のまろやかな豆乳を使い、厳選した宇治抹茶の風味が豊かなふわふわ食感のバームクーヘン。花見小路店限定商品。

Ⓞ *Gion Sakai*
ぎをんさかい
☎075-531-8878 ♀P80-B3
🚶5 minute walk from Gion Shijo Station on the Keihan line
🕚11:00-19:00, Café 11:00-17:00 (last call 16:30)
💬Open year round 7 days a week

Chocolate
チョコレート

Matcha Kit Kat, Itokyuemon

抹茶キットカット 伊藤久右衛門   *864yen*

These crispy Kit Kat wafers are coated in select matcha-flavored chocolate. Created in collaboration with a famous shop of tea from Uji, this item is only available in Kyoto.
厳選された抹茶のチョコレートで、サクサクのウエハースをコーティング。有名宇治茶の店が手掛ける京都限定商品。

Ⓞ *Itokyuemon, Kyoto Station shop*
伊藤久右衛門 京都駅前店
☎075-748-1320 ♀P72-C2
🚶3 minute walk from Kyoto Station on the JR line
🕙10:00-18:30
💬Open year round 7 days a week

29 Kaiseki Ryori | 懐石料理 |

Traditional Japanese gourmet cuisine
✿ 格式ある伝統の京都グルメ

When one speaks of *Kyo-ryori*, they are referring to a traditional form of Japanese cuisine, known as kaiseki ryori, that primarily utilizes ingredients from Kyoto and gives expression to the particular season and cultural elements that accompany it. It is usually served as a course, but sometimes comes already prepared in the form of a Kyo-bento, or lunchbox. Kyo-ryori has been gaining in popularity since 2013, when washoku(or Jpanese cuisine)was designated a form of Intangible Cultural Heritage by UNESCO.

京料理とは、主に京都の食材を使い、季節や風土を表現した懐石料理を指す。基本的にはコース仕立てだが、あらかじめ器に詰められている京弁当などもある。2013年、京料理を含む「和食」がユネスコ無形文化遺産に登録されたことで、さらに注目を集めている。

Some restaurants have a counter.
カウンター席もある

One example of a kaiseki ryori course 懐石料理の流れ

1 Sakizuke 先付
The first course is a small selection of appetizers that sets the seasonal tone of the meal.
コースの初めに出される料理で、最も季節を感じられる前菜。少しずつ何種類かの料理が並ぶ。

2 Mukozuke 向付
This will generally include sashimi and / or a vinegared or dressed dish.
一般的に、刺身や酢の物、和え物が出される。

3 Wanmono 椀物
A soup served in an individual bowl with a lid. Open the lid to enjoy the smell of the broth and the design of the lacquer bowl.
汁物。フタをした状態で出されるので、開けたときの出汁の香りや漆器の柄なども楽しめる。

4 Nimono 煮物
Vegetables, *namafu, yuba tofu*, and other ingredients are stewed separately then brought together in the single dish.
野菜や生麩、湯葉などを、それぞれ別々の鍋で煮て一つの器に盛り付けたもの。

62

5 Yakimono
焼物

This is usually grilled seasonal fish but sometimes *tempura*.

季節の焼き魚が多い。天ぷらの場合もある。

6 Mushimono
蒸物

This is a dish of steamed fish, vegetables or other ingredients. Rice is served after this dish, so people who want to drink a little more sake beforehand should tell the server to bring the rice a little later.

魚や野菜を蒸した料理。蒸物の次は御飯が出てくる。まだお酒などを楽しみたい場合は「御飯はもう少し後で」と伝えよう。

7 Rice, tsukemono pickles, tea
御飯、漬物、汁物

When rice is served, it signals the end of the meal is at hand. The sake is taken away and hot tea is served.

御飯が出されるとコースの最後というサイン。お酒は下げられ、熱いお茶が出される。

8 Mizumono
水物

The meal ends with a dessert, usually something light and simple such as a seasonal fruit or sherbet.

コースの最後に出されるデザート。季節の果物やシャーベットなど、さっぱりとしたシンプルなものが多い。

Famous Kaiseki Ryori Restaurants　懐石料理の名店

Kaiseki Ryori ● 懐石料理

Gion Kawakami　祇園川上

The owner-chef apprenticed at famous restaurants around the country and serves delicately flavored dishes that are beautifully presented.

各地の名店で修業を重ねた主人による、見た目にも美しい繊細な味の京料理が楽しめる。

Lunchtime kaiseki ryori: from 5,400yen
お昼の懐石料理 5400 円～

☎075-561-2420 (reservation required)
📍P80-B3 🚶5 minute walk from Gion-shijo Station on the Keihan Line 🕐12:00 – last call 13:30, 17:00 – last call 21:00 🈺Unscheduled

Kinobu　木乃婦

Lunchtime mini kaiseki (available only on week-days): from 5,250yen (not including tax and service)
お昼のミニ会席（平日のみ）5250 円～（税サ別）

Kyo-ryori at Kinobu features an innovative use of French cooking methods and ingredients used in Western cooking.

フランス料理の手法や西洋の食材などを取り入れた、自由で先進的な発想の京料理が味わえる。

☎075-352-0001 📍P74-C3
🚶5 minute walk from Shijo Station on the Karasuma subway line. 🕐12:00 – last call 13:00, 18:00 – last call 19:30 🈺Some Wednesdays (Check in advance)

Jiki Miyazawa　じき宮ざわ

This restaurant serves *Kyo-ryori* made from select ingredients and is a popular place to enjoy a casual meal. The toasted sesame tofu melts in your mouth and is a favorite of the patrons here.

Lunchtime course from 3,780yen
昼のコース 3780 円～

上質な素材を生かした京料理をカジュアルに楽しめる人気店。名物は口の中でとろける焼胡麻豆腐。

☎075-213-1326(reservation required)
📍P75-D3 🚶5 minute walk from Karasuma Station on the Hankyu line 🕐12:00 – last call 13:45, 17:30 – last call 20:00 🈺Thursdays and the 1st Wednesday of every month
*The adult rate applies to students in elementary school and above.

Some restaurants add a 10% service charge.　別途サービス料 10%がかかる場合もある。
Some restaurants are only open for dinner.　店によりディナーのみ営業

30

Shojin ryori

| 精進料理 |

The ultimate health food
✿ 究極のヘルシーフード

Shojin ryori is a type of vegetarian cuisine originally eaten by ascetic Buddhist monks. Meals are made using only seasonal vegetables, beans, seaweed and other plants, and neither meat nor fish is included. The dishes are served in simple, beautiful arrangements that allow the diner to savor the flavors of each ingredient. Shojin ryori is available at many temples and traditional Japanese restaurants in Kyoto.

精進料理とは、仏教の修行僧が食していた料理のこと。季節の野菜や豆、海草など植物性の食材で作られ、魚や肉類は一切使わない。シンプルに美しく盛り付けられた料理は、素材そのものの味を楽しめる。京都では、寺院や料亭などで食べることができる。

Shojin ryori, Yuki (Snow): 3,000yen
精進料理（雪）3000円

A Sesame tofu made with ground sesame paste. It has a slightly chewy consistency.
胡麻を練って作られた胡麻豆腐。もちもちした食感。

B A colorful arrangement of seasonal vegetables and chimaki-wheat-gluten cakes wrapped in bamboo leaves
旬の野菜と、生麩を笹の葉で包んだちまきを彩りよく盛り合わせたもの。

C *Gojiru* soup made by grinding soybeans into a paste called "*go*," which is then dissolved in *dashi*.
大豆をすりつぶした「呉」を出汁で溶かした汁物・呉汁。

D *Shimeji* mushrooms and spinach with a zesty accent of freshly squeezed *yuzu* juice.
香り高い柚子を搾った、しめじとほうれん草の和え物。

E Arrangement of simmered pod peas, *shiitake* mushrooms, *yubatofu*, and a doughnut-shaped piece of *kuruma-fu*.
えんどう、しいたけ、湯葉、ドーナツ状に穴の開いた車麩の煮物を盛り付けたもの。

F A dumpling made of *ebi-imo* (taro from Kyoto) served warm with a thick sauce.
京都特産のえびいもの饅頭にあんをかけた温かい料理。

G Seasonal strawberry and Mandarine orange for dessert.
デザート。旬の果物のイチゴとミカン。

H Fluffy cooked white rice (domestically grown).
ふっくらと炊き上げた国産の白米。

I Pickled radish and *shibazuke* pickles
大根の漬物、しば漬け。

Tenryu-ji Temple, Shigetsu
天龍寺 篩月

This restaurant is located on the premises of Tenryu-ji Temple. You are served a large variety of authentic shojin ryori dishes made using soup stock prepared mainly from vegetables and *shiitake* mushrooms.

天龍寺の境内にある店。野菜、シイタケから主に出汁をとった本格的な精進料理は品数豊富。

☎075-882-9725 📍P79-B3
🚶2 minute walk from Arashiyama Station on the Randen (Keifuku) Line ¥500yen to enter the gardens
🕐11:00-last call 14:00
📅Open year round 7 days a week

Seigen-in, sub-temple of Ryoan-ji Temple 龍安寺 西源院

This restaurant is located on the premises of Ryoan-ji Temple(→P22), a temple famed for its rock garden. A set meal here consists of eight shojin dishes, including rich sesame tofu and a tofu and vegetable salad, and the famous boiled tofu and vegetable dish.

石庭で有名な龍安寺（→P22）の境内にある。濃厚な胡麻豆腐や豆腐と野菜を和えた白和えなど8品の精進料理に、名物の七草湯豆腐がセットになる。

☎075-462-4742 ♥P78-A2
🚶3 minute walk from the JR Bus Ryoanji-mae bus stop
🕙10:00-last call 16:00
Open year round 7 days a week

Shojin ryori with yudofu
3,300yen
湯豆腐付きの精進料理は3300円

Izusen, Daiji-in shop
泉仙 大慈院店

Izusen first opened many years ago on the grounds of Daiji-in, a sub-temple of Daitoku-ji Temple. Dishes are served in red bowls designed to look like the iron bowls that monks use to receive donations of food.

大徳寺塔頭・大慈院内の老舗。僧侶が食べ物を受けるのに用いたという鉄鉢を模した赤い器に料理が盛り付けられる。

Shojin Teppatsu Ryori, Ayame
3,240yen for seven dishes.
精進鉄鉢料理あやめ3240円は全7品

☎075-491-6665 ♥P76-B1
🚶5 minute walk from the Kyoto City Bus Daitoku-ji-mae bus stop
🕙11:00-last call 16:00
Open year round 7 days a week

Nanzen-ji Temple, Junsei 南禅寺 順正

Visitors will find a number of restaurants selling boiled tofu, or *yudofu*, near the gates of Nanzen-ji Temple. Junsei is one of the more popular establishments, and they offer a set course meal that includes richly-flavored tofu made from soy beans grown in Japan.

南禅寺の門前には湯豆腐店が軒を連ねる。なかでも順正は人気店の一つで、国産大豆を使った濃厚な味わいの豆腐をコースで楽しめる。

☎075-761-2311 ♥P70-D3
🚶5 minute walk from Keage Station on the Tozai subway line
🕙11:00-last call 20:00
Open year round 7 days a week

Yudofu Hito-tori: 3,090yen
ゆどうふ一通り3090円

Popular wagyu beef restaurants

31

| 人気の和牛レストラン |

Eating top quality beef steek

✿ 極上のステーキを食べる

The people of Kyoto consume more beef than most cities in Japan, and the city is also one of the first places where people began eating beef when Western culture was reintroduced to Japan more than 140 years ago. Kyoto is surrounded by areas famous for wagyu, so it always has a delicious supply of beef available. Steak is recommended if you are looking to experience the essential flavor of wagyu beef.

京都は、牛肉の消費量が国内で常に上位。約140年前、西洋文化の到来とともに牛肉の食文化がいち早く広まった場所でもある。地理的に、有名な和牛の産地に囲まれているため美味しい牛肉が集まる場所ともいわれる。牛肉の醍醐味を味わえるステーキで堪能しよう。

Chic Japanese-style interior with counter and tables
シックな和の雰囲気の店内にはカウンターとテーブル席がある

Hafuu はふう

This is a popular restaurant in Kyoto that specializes in beef dishes. The owner runs a wholesale business and can therefore offer high-quality wagyu beef at reasonable prices. They have a particular method of grilling the beef in which stones that are placed under the grill cause the oil that drips down to rebound back up, thus enhancing the flavor of the beef.

京都で人気の肉料理専門店。オーナーが問屋業を営むため、リーズナブルな価格で良質な和牛を提供する。焼き方にこだわりがあり、石を下に敷いたグリルで焼くことで、落ちた油が石に当たって跳ね返り、さらに肉のうま味が増すという。

One characteristic of wagyu beef is the beauty of the fine mesh-like marbling.
脂肪が細かく網の目のように入った美しさが和牛の特徴

Excess oil drips down below the iron griddle so that even sirloin steak has a more delicate flavor.
鉄板の下に余分な油が落ち、サーロインでもあっさりとした味わいになる

Located in a quiet residential area, the unobtrusive atmosphere of the flagship restaurant has the feel of a secret hideaway.
閑静な住宅街にある、落ち着いた趣のある本店は隠れ家のようだ

☎075-257-1581 📍P75-D1
🚶10 minute walk from Marutamachi Station on the Karasuma Subway line
🕐11:30-last call 13:30, 17:30-last call 21:30
🈺Wednesdays

Premium beef sirloin steak 150g, 4,800yen. A little *dashi* soy sauce adds subtle flavors and garlic chips are placed on top. It comes with three kinds of dipping sauces, including one made from white *miso* and *ponzu*.
At lunchtime, it costs 4,500yen and comes with a side dish, salad, rice, miso soup, pickled vegetables and coffee.
極上牛サーロインステーキ150g 4800円。隠し味に出汁醤油を少々、にんにくチップをのせて食べる。白味噌ポン酢など、お好みで3種類のソースも付けて。ランチは小鉢、サラダ、ご飯、みそ汁、香物、コーヒー付で4500円

There are about 30 seats including counter seats and those in a straw-mat area at large tables that may be shared with other diners.
合い席にもなる大机の座敷席とカウンター席で約30席ほどある

Murasawa beef sirloin steak set with rice and a small salad, 5,900yen (150g).
村沢牛サーロインステーキ150g（ライス・ミニサラダ付）5900円

Otsuka おおつか

This restaurant carries Murasawa beef, a rarely seen brand from Nagano prefecture. It is also quite unusual for a brand of wagyu beef to be named after the producer. The rich savory flavor is characteristic of high-class beef, and it's so tender you don't even need a knife to cut it.
幻といわれる長野県の村沢牛を扱う店。生産者名がブランド名となった珍しい和牛。高級牛ならではの豊かなコクとうま味が特徴で、ナイフが要らないほどのやわらかさだ。

☎075-864-7989 ♥P79-C3
🚶5 minute walk from Saga Arashi-yama Station on the JR line
🕐11:00-15:00 (last call 14:30)
🚫Thursdays

This restaurant is located in a residential area off the main street that stretches from Togetsu-kyo Bridge.
渡月橋から延びる大通りから外れた住宅街にある

Steak House Pound
ステーキハウス 听（ぽんど）

This restaurant specializes in wagyu beef that has undergone dry-aging, a traditional process used in the West. Head down to the dry-aging cellar to choose the cut of beef you are looking for. They serve only domestic Japanese black wagyu, and it is carefully grilled over a charcoal fire so that even the leaner portions of the meat are tender and flavorful.
欧米の伝統技法・ドライエイジングされた熟成和牛の専門店。店頭にある熟成肉セラーから好みの部位を選んで注文できる。国産黒毛和牛にこだわり、炭火で丁寧に焼き上げられた牛肉は赤身部分までやわらかく凝縮された牛肉のうま味が味わえる。

Dry-aged wagyu beef sirloin steak 1/2 pound (225g) is served for lunch with rice, *miso* soup and salad for 4,560yen, and for dinner a la carte for 5,170yen.
熟成和牛サーロインステーキ1/2ポンド（225g）は、ランチ4560円でごはん、みそ汁、サラダ付。ディナーは単品で5170円

A 100 year old Kyoto-style townhouse with small courtyard garden was renovated for this restaurant location.
築100年以上の京町家を改装した店。坪庭もある

☎075-708-6110 ♥P74-C1
🚶2 minute walk from Marutamachi Station on the Karasuma Subway line
🕐11:30-14:30 (last call 14:00), 17:00-23:00 (last call 22:30)
🚫Mondays

Beef on display has been aged for 40 to 45 days under strict quality management.
徹底的な品質管理のもと、40〜45日間かけて熟成させた牛肉が並ぶ

32

Ramen ｜ラーメン｜

The king of "B class" cuisine
☙ B級グルメの王様

Ramen is perhaps the most well known kind of Japanese "B class" cuisine, and Kyoto is a veritable battleground of ramen shops, including both long-established ramen restaurants and those offering more innovative types of ramen. There are many popular restaurants that have lines to get in, and sometimes they even run out of food part way through business hours. The combination of noodles, soup and toppings in ramen makes for a variety of restaurants, and its fun to go searching for the kinds of Kyoto ramen you like the most.

ラーメンは日本を代表するB級グルメ。京都は老舗からニューウェーブまでが集まる激戦区だ。行列ができる人気店も多く、売り切れてしまうこともある。麺とスープ、さまざまな具を組み合わせたラーメンは、店ごとに特徴があるので、自分好みの京都ラーメンを探そう。

Menma　メンマ
Crispy slices of flavored bamboo shoots.
原材料は竹の子。しゃきしゃきした噛みごたえ

Men　麺
The noodles are thin and straight, and you can choose the hardness.
細めのストレート。麺のかたさを選ぶことができる

Soup　スープ
The white chicken broth with a soy sauce base is characteristic of traditional Kyoto ramen.
すっきりとしたキレのある醤油のタレに、鶏ガラを炊き込んだ白湯スープが元祖京都ラーメン

Chashu　チャーシュー
String is tightly wound around a thick cut of pork that is simmered and then thinly sliced.
塊の豚肉を糸で固く縛り、煮込んだものを薄くスライス

Negi　ネギ
Kujo-negi, a traditional Kyoto vegetable, is generally used for this condiment. The soy-sauce-based soup enhances the sweetness of the green onion.
薬味。伝統的な京野菜の九条ネギを使用。醤油スープがネギの甘味を引き出す

Se-abura　背脂
Se-abura refers to pork backfat that after being slowly simmered is pressed through a mesh strainer and collected in a bowl. It adds a pleasant sweetness and enhances the flavor of the soup. Ramen with se-abura is one of the primary styles of Kyoto ramen.
じっくりと煮込んだ豚の脂身の塊をざるに入れて、鉢の上で押しつぶした脂の粒のこと。スープの甘味とうま味が増す。背脂入りは京都のラーメンの一つの主流スタイル

ramen : 650yen
ラーメン　650 円

Masutani　ますたに
Masutani was the first ramen restaurant that offered ramen in a soy-sauce soup topped with se-abura. A generous amount of se-abura is added to this chicken-bone broth gently accented with spicy red pepper, but the soup is unexpectedly light.

背脂醤油ラーメンの元祖。たっぷりと背脂が入る鶏がらスープにピリッと辛い一味がアクセント。意外にあっさりとしている。

☎075-781-5762　📍P70-D3
🚶 Near the Kyoto City Bus Ginkakuji-michi bus stop ⏰ 10:00 – 19:00, until 18:00 on Sundays and holidays (closes when the ramen is sold out) 📅 Mondays and the 3rd Tuesday of every month

Tenka Ippin 天下一品

One of the most famous richly flavored types of ramen. The thick *kotteri* soup broth is made by boiling chicken bones, more than ten kinds of vegetables, and other ingredients, making it like a rich cream soup. This flagship restaurant is the first store among more than 230 branches inside and outside Japan.

濃厚ラーメンの代表。鶏ガラと十数種類の野菜などから作られたこってりスープは、ポタージュのように濃厚な味わい。ここ本店は国内外230店舗以上ある中の第1号店。

☎075-722-0955 ♥P70-D3
🚶3 minute walk from the Kyoto City Bus Ichijoji-kinomoto-cho bus stop ⏰11:00 – 3:00 on the next day 🚫Thursdays

Kotteri (Thick-soup) ramen (regular size) : 700yen
こってりラーメン（並）700 円

Shinpukusaikan 新福菜館

The broth made from boiled pork and chicken bones is given a dark color and tasty accent from soy sauce, but the flavor is mild enough to drink. The same soup also goes into making their famous fried rice (500yen).

豚骨と鶏ガラをベースに色の濃い醤油による香ばしいタレで味付けしたスープは、マイルドなので飲み干せる美味しさ。同じスープで作った焼き飯500円も名物。

☎075-371-7648 ♥P72-C2
🚶5 minute walk from Kyoto Station on the JR line
⏰7:30 – 22:00 🚫Wednesdays

Chuka-soba : 700yen
中華そば 700 円

Honke Daiichi Asahi Takabashi

本家第一旭 たかばし

They got their start about 50 years ago, and their ramen is characterized by a full-bodied yet clear pork-bone broth. The bowl is blanketed by generous amounts of kujo-negi green onions, bean sprouts and sliced roast pork.

創業約50年。コクのある透明な豚骨スープが特徴。たっぷりの九条ネギとモヤシ、チャーシューが鉢を覆うほどのっている。

Tokusei Ramen : 850yen
特製ラーメン 850 円

☎075-351-6321 ♥P72-C2
🚶5 minute walk from Kyoto Station on the JR line ⏰5:30 – 2:00 on the next day 🚫Thursdays

At Kyoto Station, you'll find a selection of famous ramen restaurants from throughout the country
京都駅に全国の有名店が集合

Kyoto Ramen Koji 京都拉麺小路

Located on the 10th floor of Kyoto Staion Building. There are 8 ramen restaurants to choose from spanning the nation from Hokkaido to Kyushu. Masutani has a branch here as well.

京都駅ビル10Fにあるコーナー。北海道から九州まで、日本全国の名店8軒のラーメンが食べられる。「ますたに」の支店もある。

☎Varies by store ♥P72-C2
🚶Near Kyoto Station on the JR line
⏰11:00 – 22:00 (Last call 21:30)
🚫Unscheduled

The Greatest Travel Tips **Kyoto**

70

N

0 2km

To Ohara 大原へ→ ★
Hosen-in Temple 宝泉院

Kurama-dera Temple 鞍馬寺
Kurama hot spring くらま温泉
Kurama-no-hi Matsuri 鞍馬の火祭 P100
Kurama Sta. 鞍馬駅
由岐神社 Yuki-jinja Shrine
Kibune-guchi Sta. 貴船口駅
Kibune-jinja Shrine 貴船神社

Kurama 鞍馬

Ninose Sta. 二ノ瀬駅
貴船川 Eizan Ry. Kurama Line 叡山電鉄鞍馬線

Kibunegawa River

Ichihara Sta. 市原駅
Niken-jaya Sta. 二軒茶屋駅
Kino 木野
Kyoto Seika Dai-mae Sta. 京都精華大前駅
Aoi Matsuri 葵祭 P98
Kamo-Kurabe-uma 賀茂競馬 P98

Gozan no Okuribi(Funagata) 五山送り火(船形) P99
Gozan no Okuribi(Myo) 五山送り火(妙) P99
Genko-an Temple 源光庵
Gozan no Okuribi(Ho) 五山送り火(法) P99

Gozan no Okuribi(Hidari Daimonji) 五山送り火(左大文字) P99
Imamiya-jinja Shrine 今宮神社

Gozan no Okuribi(Torigata) 五山送り火(鳥居形) P99

Takao 高雄
Saimyo-ji Temple 西明寺 P9
高山寺 Kosan-ji Temple
Jingo-ji Temple 神護寺
嵐山高雄 Arashiyama Takao Parkway 嵐山高雄パークウエイ

Sagano 嵯峨野
Otaginenbutsu-ji Temple 愛宕念仏寺
Torokko Hozukyo Sta. トロッコ保津峡駅 保津峡駅
To Torokko Kameoka Sta. 亀岡駅
Hozu-kyo Sta. 保津峡駅

Saga Arashiyama Sta. 嵯峨嵐山駅
Rokuo-ji Sta. 鹿王院駅
Arashiyama Sta. 嵐山駅

Jisso-in Temple 実相院
Kurama River

Ichihara 貫流川

Entsu-ji Temple 圓通寺
Iwakura Sta. 岩倉駅
Takaragaike Sta. 宝ヶ池駅
Kitayama-dori 北山通
京都府立植物園 Kyoto Botanical Garden
Ichijoji Sta. 一乗寺駅
Shinogamo-dori 下鴨神社 Shimogamo-jinja Shrine

Kamigamo-Jinja Shinto Shrine 上賀茂神社 P8・31
上賀茂神社前 Kamigamo-jinja-mae

Takaragaike Sta. 宝ヶ池駅

Hachiman-mae Sta. 八幡前駅
Hachiman Sta. 八幡駅
Miyake Hachiman Sta. 三宅八幡駅
Yase Hieizan-guchi Sta. 八瀬比叡山口駅
Keifuku Cable Ry. ケーブル
Keifuku Ry. Eizan Line 叡山電鉄本線
叡山電鉄鞍馬線

Shugakuin Sta. 修学院駅
Shugakuin Imperial Villa 修学院離宮 P35

Chayama Sta. 茶山駅

Takanogawa River 高野川

Enpyaku-ji Temple P8 円山寺
延暦寺
Keifuku Cable Ry. ケーブル
叡山ロープウエイ Hieizan Ropeway
Hieizan Driveway 比叡山ドライブウエイ
比叡山

Shisen-do Temple 詩仙堂 P47
詩仙堂

Shugaku-in Sta. 修学院駅
Shugakuin Imperial Villa

Tenka Ippin 天下一品 P69 Masutani まるすたに P68
一乗寺下り松町 Ichijoji-sagarimatsu-cho
Ginkaku-ji Temple(Jisho-ji Temple) 銀閣寺(慈照寺) P9-15
Mototanaka Sta. 元田中駅 銀閣寺道 Ginkakuji-michi
Shinnyodo Temple 真正極楽寺(真如堂) P19
Shirakawa-dori 白川通
Shugakuin-Hikyu-michi 一乗寺木ノ本町
Honen-in Temple 法然院
Shirakawa-dori 白川通
Demachi-yanagi Sta. 出町柳駅
Marutamachi Sta. 丸太町駅
Shinnyodo Temple 真正極楽寺(真如堂)
Eikan-do Temple(Zenrin-ji Temple) 永観堂(禅林寺) P99
Konkai komyo-ji Temple 金戒光明寺 P78
Gozan no Okuribi (Daimonji) 五山送り火(大文字)
Gozan no Okuribi (Daimonji) 五山送り火(大文字) P99

Kamogawa River 鴨川
Imadegawa-dori 今出川通
Shinmachi-dori 新町通

Kitaoji-dori 北大路通
P74-75
Kyoto Imperial Palace 京都御所 P8
京都御苑
P76-77
Senbon-dori 千本通
Nijo-jo Castle 二条城 P46
二条城
Nijo Sta. 二条駅
Horikawa-dori 堀川通

Kitano Hakubai-cho Sta. 北野白梅町駅
Kitano-jinja Shrine
Keifuku Ry. 京福北野線
Enmachi Sta. 円町駅
Hanazono Sta. 花園駅
P78
Keifuku Ry. Kitano Line 京福北野線
Narutaki 鳴滝駅
Utano Sta. 宇多野駅
Uzumasa Sta. 太秦駅
Uzumasa Koryu-ji Sta. 太秦広隆寺駅
Toei Kyoto Studio Park 東映太秦映画村 P42
東映太秦映画村
Kurumazaki-jinja Shrine 車折神社
JR San-in Line JR山陰本線
Keifuku Ry. Keifuku Ry.

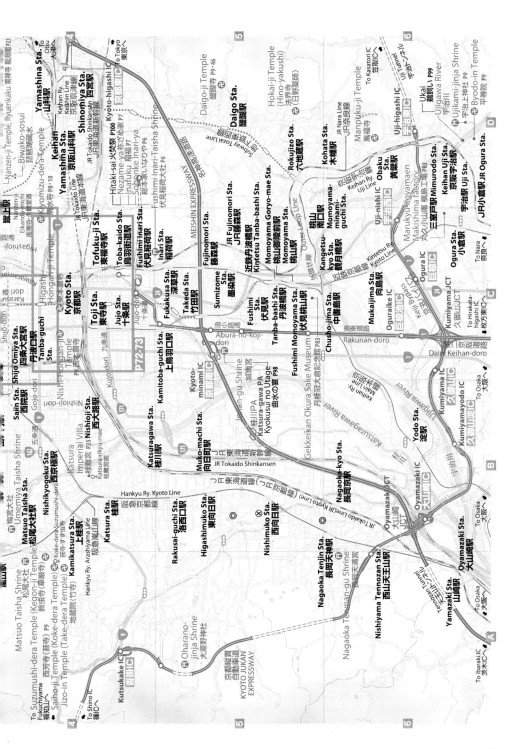

嵯峨嵐山駅へ
To Saga Arashiyama Sta.

四条堀川へ
To Shijo Horikawa

烏丸駅へ
To Karasuma Sta.

Horikawa Gojo
堀川五条

Karasuma Gojo
烏丸五条

Karasuma Gojo

西京極へ
To Nishi-
kyogoku

**Tanba-guchi
Sta.
丹波口駅**

Central
Wholesale
Market
中央卸売市場

京都東急ホテル
Kyoto Tokyu Hotel

烏丸五条
**Gojo Sta.
五条駅**

鍵屋町通
Kagiya-cho-dori

Higashi-no-toin-dori

西洞院通

上珠数屋町
Kamijuzuya-
machi-do

Central
Wholesale
Market
中央
卸売市場

花屋町通

Hanaya-cho-dori

**Higashi
Hongan-ji
Temple**
東本願寺

下珠数屋町
Shimojuzu-
machi-do

Nishi Honganji-mae
西本願寺前

Nishi Hongan-ji Temple
西本願寺 P9

Shomen-dori
正面通

堀川通

Wakamiya-dori

Nishi-no-toin-dori

七条大宮

Shichijo Omiya
七条大宮

Omiya-dori
大宮通

Mibugawa-dori
壬生川通

七条堀川

Shichijo Horikawa
七条堀川

Horikawa-dori
堀川通

Karasuma Shichijo
烏丸七条

Shichijo-d

**Itokyuemon, Kyoto Station shop
伊藤久右衛門 京都駅前店** P61

Books Sanseido,
Kyoto Station branch
三省堂書店京都駅店

**Kyoto Tower
京都タワー**

Kyoto Railway Museum
京都鉄道博物館

Midori-no-yakata
緑の館

Umekoji Park
梅小路公園

Rihga Royal Hotel Kyoto
リーガロイヤル
ホテル京都

Kyoto New-hankyu Hotel
京都新阪急ホテル

Biccamera JR Kyoto
Station branch
ビックカメラJR京都駅店

JR Kyoto Isetan Dept.
ジェイアール
京都伊勢丹

Kyoto
Century Hotel
京都
センチュリー
ホテル

Kyoto
Sta.BT

Kyoto Ramen Koji
京都拉麺小路 P69

**Kyoto Sta.
京都駅** P94

ホテル
グランヴィア京都
Hotel Granvia Kyoto

京都駅

Roku-sonno-jinja Shrine
六孫王神社

八条通

Hachijo-dori

New Miyako Hotel
新・都ホテル

Avanti
アバンティ

大阪へ
To Osaka

New Miyako Hotel
South Wing
新・都ホテル
サウスウィング

Shinpukusaika
新福菜館

Honke Dai
本家第一旭
Takaba
たかば

終い弘法 P101
Shimai Kobo
(Gift shop on the temple grounds)
東寺(境内売店) P60

P8・27

**Toji Temple
(Kyo-o-gokoku-ji)
Temple)**
東寺(教王護国寺)

**Toji Sta.
東寺駅**
Kujo Abura-no-koji
九条油小路

Kujo-dori

Goju-no-to
五重塔

Rajo-mon-ato
羅城門跡

長岡京へ
To Nagaoka-kyo

Keihan-kokudo-guchi
京阪国道口

九条通
Kujo-dori

**Kujo Sta.
九条駅**

Abura-no-koji-dori
油小路通

Kintetsu Ry. Kyoto Line
近鉄京都線

Shinmachi-dori
新町通

Muromachi-dori
室町通

Subway Karasuma Line
地下鉄烏丸線

Karasuma-dori
烏丸通

Takeda-kaido
竹田街道

札ノ辻通
Fuda-no-tsuji-dori

N

200m

To Hirakata
枚方へ

To Takeda Sta.
竹田駅へ

To Takeda Sta.
竹田駅へ

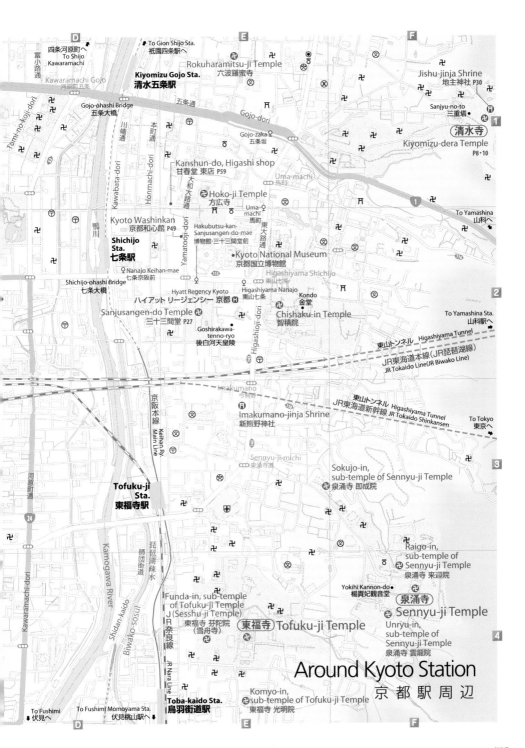

D | **E** | **F**

四条河原町へ
To Shijo
Kawaramachi

To Gion Shijo Sta.
祇園四条駅へ

Rokuharamitsu-ji Temple
六波羅蜜寺

Jishu-jinja Shrine
地主神社 P30

Tomi-no-koji-dori
富小路通

Kawaramachi Gojo
河原町五条

Kiyomizu Gojo Sta.
清水五条駅

Sanjyu-no-to
三重塔

1

Gojo-ohashi Bridge
五条大橋

五条通
Gojo-dori

Gojo-zaka
五条坂

清水寺
Kiyomizu-dera Temple
P8·10

川端通

本町通

Kanshun-do, Higashi shop
甘春堂 東店 P59

Uma-machi
馬町

Kawabata-dori

大和大路通

Honmachi-dori

Hoko-ji Temple
方広寺

To Yamashina
山科へ

1

Kyoto Washinkan
京都和心館 P49

Hakubutsu-kan-
Sanjusangen-do-mae
博物館・三十三間堂前

Uma-
machi
馬町

東大路通

**Shichijo
Sta.**
七条駅

Yamatooji-dori
大和大路通

Kyoto National Museum
京都国立博物館

Higashiyama Shichijo
東山七条

2

Nanajo Keihan-mae
七条京阪前

Higashiyama Nanajo
東山七条

Kondo
金堂

To Yamashina Sta.
山科駅へ

Shichijo-ohashi Bridge
七条大橋

Hyatt Regency Kyoto
ハイアット リージェンシー 京都

Chishaku-in Temple
智積院

鴨川

Sanjusangen-do Temple
三十三間堂 P27

Goshirakawa-
tenno-ryo
後白河天皇陵

Higashiyama-dori
東山通

東山トンネル Higashiyama Tunnel

JR東海道本線（JR琵琶湖線）
JR Tokaido Line(JR Biwako Line)

京阪本線
Keihan Ry.
Main Line

Imakumano
今熊野

東山トンネル Higashiyama Tunnel
JR東海道新幹線 JR Tokaido Shinkansen

To Tokyo
東京へ

Imakumano-jinja Shrine
新熊野神社

3

Sennyu-ji-michi
泉涌寺道

Sokujo-in,
sub-temple of Sennyu-ji Temple
泉涌寺 即成院

**Tofuku-ji
Sta.**
東福寺駅

Kawaramachi-dori
河原町通

Raigo-in,
sub-temple of
Sennyu-ji Temple
泉涌寺 来迎院

24

Biwako-sosui
琵琶湖疏水

師団街道
Shidan-kaido

Yokihi Kannon-do
楊貴妃観音堂

泉涌寺
Sennyu-ji Temple

Funda-in, sub-temple
of Tofuku-ji Temple
J (Sesshu-ji Temple)
東福寺 芬陀院
（雪舟寺）

東福寺 Tofuku-ji Temple

Unryu-in,
sub-temple of
Sennyu-ji Temple
泉涌寺 雲龍院

4

Kamogawa River
鴨川

Biwako-sosui
琵琶湖疏水

JR奈良線
JR Nara Line

Around Kyoto Station
京都駅周辺

Komyo-in,
sub-temple of Tofuku-ji Temple
東福寺 光明院

Toba-kaido Sta.
鳥羽街道駅

To Fushimi
伏見へ

To Fushimi Momoyama Sta.
伏見桃山駅へ

D | **E** | **F**

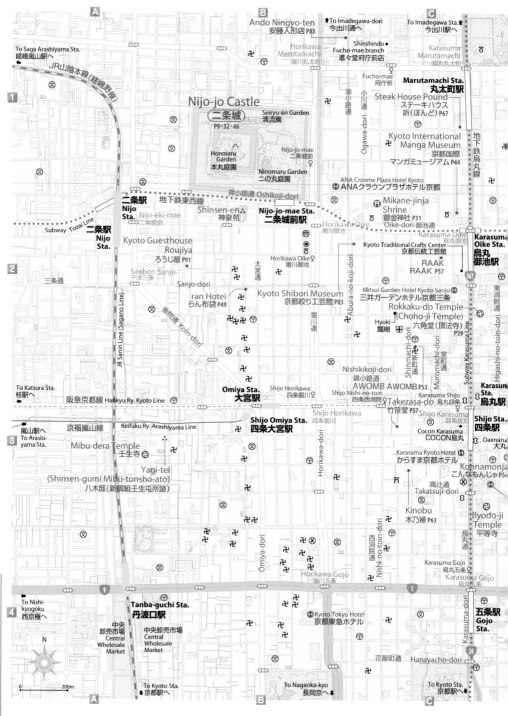

Ando Ningyo-ten
安藤人形店 P83

↑To Imadegawa-dori
今出川通へ

Shinshindo
Fucho-mae branch
進々堂府庁前店

↑To Imadegawa Sta.
今出川駅へ

Horikawa
Marutamachi
堀川丸太町

Karasuma
Marutamachi
烏丸丸太町

Fucho-mae
府庁前

油小路通

小川通

Marutamachi Sta.
丸太町駅

Steak House Pound
ステーキハウス
听(ぽんど) P67

Kyoto International
Manga Museum
京都国際
マンガミュージアム P44

地下鉄烏丸線

To Saga Arashiyama Sta.
嵯峨嵐山駅へ

JR山陰本線(嵯峨野線)
JR Sanin Line

Nijo-jo Castle
二条城
P9・32・46

Seiryu-en Garden
清流園

Nijo-jo-mae
二条城前

Honmaru
Garden
本丸庭園

Ninomaru Garden
二の丸庭園

ANA Crowne Plaza Hotel Kyoto
ANAクラウンプラザホテル京都

Mikane-jinja
Shrine
御金神社 P31

押小路通 Oshikoji-dori

二条駅
Nijo
Sta.

地下鉄東西線

Nijo-jo-mae Sta.
二条城前駅

Oike-dori 御池通

Nijo-eki-mae
二条駅前

Subway Tozai Line

二条駅
Nijo
Sta.

Shinsen-en
神泉苑

Horikawa Oike
堀川御池

Karasuma
Oike Sta.
烏丸
御池駅

Kyoto Traditional Crafts Center
京都伝統工芸館

RAAK
RAAK P57

Kyoto Guesthouse
Roujiya
ろうじ屋 P91

Senbon Sanjo
千本三条

三条通

Sanjo-dori

大宮通

Horikawa Oike
堀川御池

Mitsui Garden Hotel Kyoto Sanjo
三井ガーデンホテル京都三条

ran Hotei
らん布袋 P49

後院通 Koin-dori

堀川通

Kyoto Shibori Museum
京都絞り工芸館

Rokkaku-do Temple
(Choho-ji Temple)
六角堂(頂法寺)
P29

Hyoki
瓢樹

東洞院通

Abura-no-koji-dori

Shinmachi-dori 新町通

宮川通

Muromachi-dori

Higashi-no-toin-dori

Subway Karasuma Line

JR Sanin Line (Sagano Line)

Nishikikoji-dori
錦小路通

AWOMB AWOMB P53

Omiya Sta.
大宮駅

Shijo Horikawa
四条堀川

Shijo Nishi-no-toin
四条西洞院

Takezasa-do
竹笹堂 P57

Karasuma Shijo
烏丸四条

Karasuma
Sta.
烏丸駅

阪急京都線 Hankyu Ry. Kyoto Line

Shijo Horikawa
四条堀川

Shijo Karasuma
四条烏丸

Shijo Karasuma
四条駅

To Katsura Sta.
桂駅へ

Shijo Omiya Sta.
四条大宮駅

Cocon Karasuma
COCON烏丸

Daimaru
大丸

嵐山駅へ
To Arashi-
yama Sta.

京福嵐山線

Keifuku Ry. Arashiyama Line

Mibu-dera Temple
壬生寺

Karasuma Kyoto Hotel
からすま京都ホテル

Konnamonja
こんなもんじゃ P5

Yagi-tei
(Shinsen-gumi Mibu-tonsho-ato)
八木邸(新選組壬生屯所跡)

堀川通
Horikawa-dori

高辻通
Takatsuji-dori

Byodo-ji
Temple
平等院

Kinobu
木乃婦 P63

烏丸通

西洞院通

Omiya-dori

Horikawa Gojo
堀川五条

Nishi-no-toin-dori

Karasuma Gojo
烏丸五条

Karasuma Gojo
烏丸五条

Karasuma-dori

To Nishi-
kyogoku
西京極へ

Tanba-guchi Sta.
丹波口駅

中央
卸売市場
Central
Wholesale
Market

中央卸売市場
Central
Wholesale
Market

Kyoto Tokyu Hotel
京都東急ホテル

Gojo
Sta.
五条駅

N

To Nagaoka-kyo
長岡京へ

花屋町通

Hanayacho-dori

To Kyoto Sta.
京都駅へ

To Kyoto Sta.
京都駅へ

0 200m

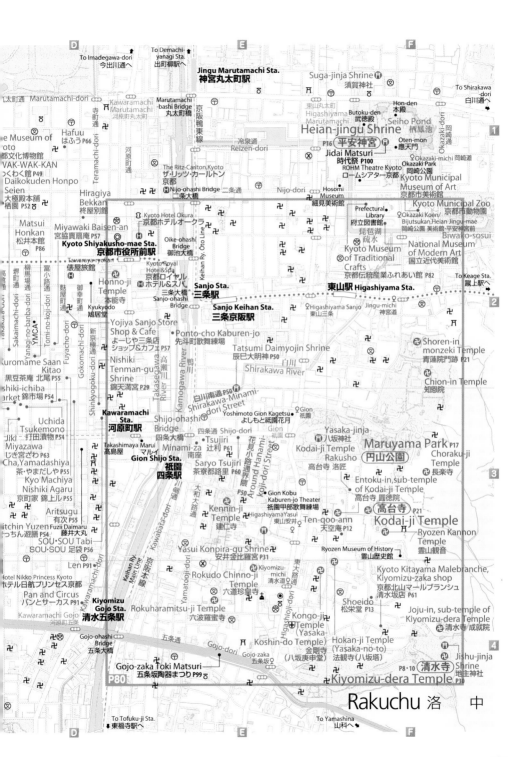

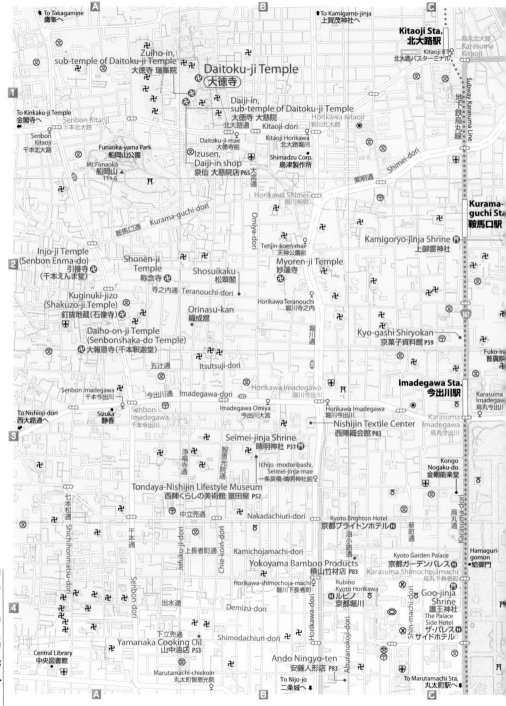

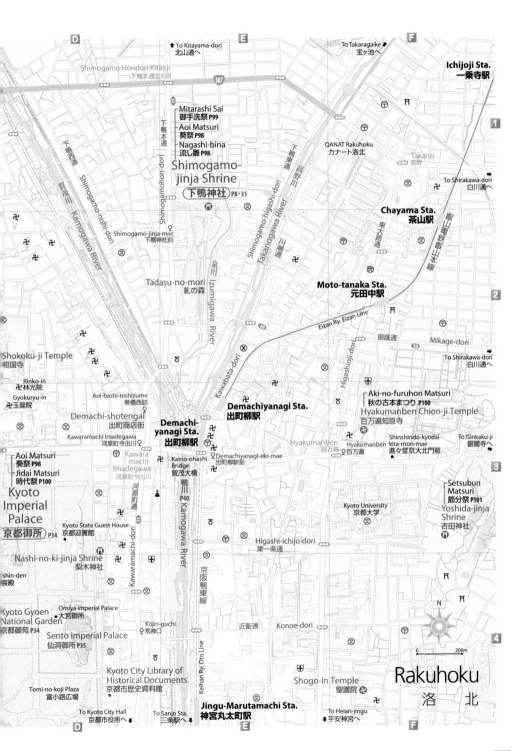

↑ To Kitayama-dori
北山通へ

↑ To Takaragaike
宝ヶ池へ

Ichijoji Sta.
一乗寺駅

Shimogamo Hondori Kitaoji
下鴨本通北大路

Mitarashi Sai
御手洗祭 P99
Aoi Matsuri
葵祭 P98
Nagashi-bina
流し雛 P98

**Shimogamo-
jinja Shrine**
下鴨神社 P8・31

QANAT Rakuhoku
カナート洛北

Takano
高野

→ To Shirakawa-dori
白川通へ

Chayama Sta.
茶山駅

Shimogamo-jinja-mae
下鴨神社前

Tadasu-no-mori
糺の森

Moto-tanaka Sta.
元田中駅

Eizan Ry. Eizan Line

Mikage-dori

→ To Shirakawa-dori
白川通へ

Shokoku-ji Temple
相国寺

Rinko-in
林光院
Gyokuryu-in
玉龍院

Aoi-bashi-nishizume
葵橋西詰

Demachiyanagi Sta.
出町柳駅

Aki-no-furuhon Matsuri
秋の古本まつり P100
Hyakumanben Chion-ji Temple
百万遍知恩寺

Demachi-shotengai
出町商店街
Kawaramachi Imadegawa
河原町今出川

**Demachi-
yanagi Sta.**
出町柳駅

Hyakumanben
百万遍

Shinshindo-kyodai-
kita-mon-mae
進々堂京大北門前

→ To Ginkaku-ji
銀閣寺へ

Hyakumanben
百万遍

Aoi Matsuri
葵祭 P98
Jidai Matsuri
時代祭 P100

**Kyoto
Imperial
Palace**
京都御所 P34

Kawara-
machi-
Imadegawa
河原町今出川

Kamo-ohashi
Bridge
賀茂大橋

Demachiyanagi-eki-mae
出町柳駅前

Kyoto University
京都大学

Setsubun
Matsuri
節分祭 P101
**Yoshida-jinja
Shrine**
吉田神社

Kyoto State Guest House
京都迎賓館

Nashi-no-ki-jinja Shrine
梨木神社

Higashi-ichijo-dori
東一条通

shin-den
殿

**Kyoto Gyoen
National Garden**
京都御苑 P34

Omiya Imperial Palace
大宮御所

Kojin-guchi
荒神口

Konoe-dori

N

Sento Imperial Palace
仙洞御所 P35

**Kyoto City Library of
Historical Documents**
京都市歴史資料館

Shogo-in Temple
聖護院

0   200m

Tomi-no-koji Plaza
富小路広場

Rakuhoku
洛　北

↑ To Kyoto City Hall
京都市役所へ

↑ To Sanjo Sta.
三条駅へ

Jingu-Marutamachi Sta.
神宮丸太町駅

↓ To Heian-jingu
平安神宮へ

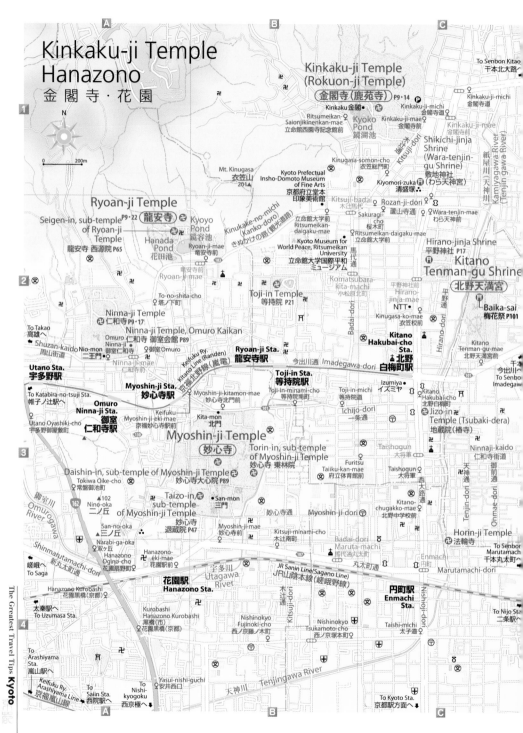

Kinkaku-ji Temple
Hanazono
金閣寺・花園

N

0   200m

**Kinkaku-ji Temple
(Rokuon-ji Temple)**
金閣寺（鹿苑寺）P9・14

To Senbon Kitao
千本北大路へ

Kinkaku-ji-michi
金閣寺道

Kinkaku-ji 金閣
Ritsumeikan-mae
立命館西園寺記念館へ
Saionjikinenkan-mae

Kinkaku-ji-mae
金閣寺前

Kinkaku-ji-michi
金閣寺道

Kinkaku-ji-mae
金閣寺前

Kyoko
Pond
鏡湖池

**Shikichi-jinja
Shrine
(Wara-tenjin-
gu Shrine)**
敷地神社（わら天神宮）

Mt. Kinugasa
衣笠山 201▲

Kyoto Prefectural
Insho-Domoto Museum
of Fine Arts
京都府立堂本
印象美術館

Kinugasa-somon-cho
衣笠総門町

Kiyomori-zuka
清盛塚●

Rozan-ji-dori
蘆山寺通

Sakuragi-
cho
桜木町

Wara-tenjin-mae
わら天神前

Ryoan-ji Temple
Seigen-in, sub-temple P9・22 龍安寺
of Ryoan-ji
Temple
龍安寺 西源院 P65

Kyoyo
Pond
鏡容池

Hanada
Pond
花田池

Ryoan-ji-mae
竜安寺前

Kinkake-no-michi
(Kanko-doro)
きぬかけの路（観光道路）

立命館大学前
Ritsumeikan-
daigaku-mae

Kyoto Museum for
World Peace, Ritsumeikan
University
立命館大学国際平和
ミュージアム

Ritsumeikan-daigaku-mae
立命館大学前

Ba-
dai-
dori
馬
代
通

Hirano-jinja Shrine
平野神社 P17

**Kitano
Tenman-gu Shrine**

Ryoan-ji-mae
竜安寺前

To-no-shita-cho
塔ノ下町

Toji-in Temple
等持院 P21

Komatsubara-
kita-machi
小松原北町

Hirano-
jinja-mae
平野神社前

北野天満宮

Ninna-ji Temple
仁和寺 P9・17

Ninna-ji Temple, Omuro Kaikan
Omuro 仁和寺 御室会館 P89
Ninna-ji 仁和寺
Nio-mon
二王門
Ninna-ji-mae

Kitano
Hirano-tsuji
平野通

NTT●

Kinugasa-ko-mae
衣笠校前

Baika-sai
梅花祭 P101

Kitano
Tenman-gu-mae
北野天満宮前

Utano Sta.
宇多野駅

Keifuku Ry.
Kitano Line (Randen)
京福北野線（嵐電）

Ryoan-ji Sta.
龍安寺駅

今出川通 Imadegawa-dori

**Kitano
Hakubai-cho
Sta.**
北野
白梅町駅

Izumiya
イズミヤ

Kitano
Hakubai-cho
北野白梅町

今出川
To Senbon
Imadegawa

To Katabira-no-tsuji Sta.
帷子ノ辻駅へ

Myoshin-ji Sta.
妙心寺駅

Myoshin-ji-kitamon-mae
妙心寺北門前

Toji-in Sta.
等持院駅

Toji-in-michi
等持院道

Toji-in-mae
等持院南町

Ichijo-dori
一条通

Jizo-in
Temple (Tsubaki-dera)
地蔵院（椿寺）

**Omuro
Ninna-ji Sta.**
御室
仁和寺駅

Keifuku
Myoshin-ji-eki-mae
京福妙心寺駅前

Kita-mon
北門

Taishogun
大将軍

Ninnaji-kaido
仁和寺街道

Utano Oyashiki-cho
宇多野御屋敷町

Myoshin-ji Temple
妙心寺

Torin-in, sub-temple
of Myoshin-ji Temple
妙心寺 東林院

Furitsu
Taiiku-kan-mae
府立体育館前

Taishogun
大将軍

Kitano-
chugakko-mae
北野中学校前

天神通 Tenjin-dori

御前通 Onmae-dori

Daishin-in, sub-temple of Myoshin-ji Temple
妙心寺大心院 P89
Tokiwa Oike-cho
常盤御池町

San-mon
三門

Myoshin-ji-dori
妙心寺通

Horin-ji Temple
法輪寺

御室川
Omuro
gawa
River

▲102
Nino-oka
二ノ丘

**Taizo-in,
sub-temple
of Myoshin-ji Temple**
妙心寺
退蔵院 P47

Myoshin-ji-mae
妙心寺前

Kitsuji-minami-cho
木辻南町

Badai-dori
Maruta-machi
馬代丸太町

Emmachi
円町

Marutamachi-dori
千本丸太町

San-no-oka
三ノ丘

Narabi-ga-oka
双ヶ丘

Hanazono
Ogino-cho
花園荻野町

Hanazono-
eki-mae
花園駅前

Maruta-machi
丸太町通

To Senbon
Marutamach
千本丸太町

Shinmarutamachi-dori
新丸太町通

To Saga
嵯峨へ

宇多川
Utagawa
River

JR Sanin Line (Sagano Line)
JR山陰本線（嵯峨野線）

**円町駅
Enmachi
Sta.**

To Nijo Sta
二条駅へ

Hanazono Kurobashi
花園黒橋（京都）

Kurobashi
Hanazono Kurobashi
黒橋（市）

**花園駅
Hanazono Sta.**

Nishinokyo
Fujinoki-cho
西ノ京藤ノ木町

Nishinokyo
Tsukamoto-cho
西ノ京塚本町

Taishi-michi
太子道

To Kyoto Sta.
京都駅方面へ

To Uzumasa Sta.
太秦駅へ

To Arashiyama
Sta.
嵐山駅へ

Keifuku Ry.
Arashiyama Line
京福嵐山線

To
Saiin Sta.
西院駅へ

To
Nishi-
kyogoku
西京極へ

Yasui-nishi-guchi
安井西口

Tenjingawa River
天神川

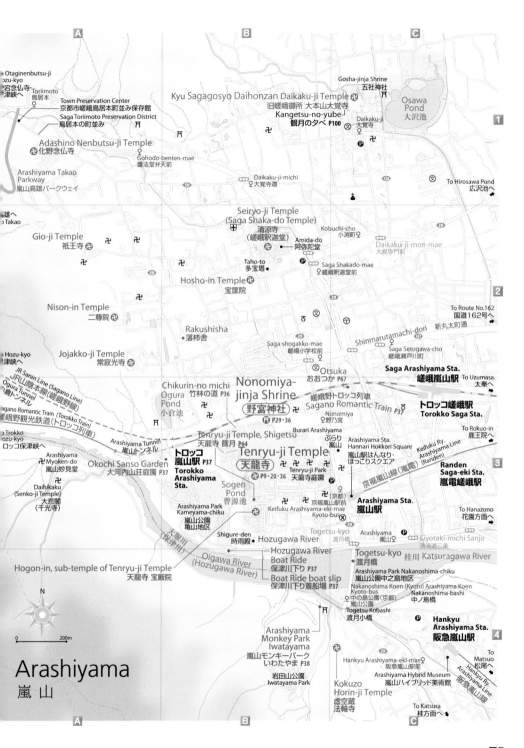

Otaginenbutsu-ji
愛宕念仏寺
hozu-kyo へ
保津峡へ

Toriimoto
鳥居本

Town Preservation Center
京都市嵯峨鳥居本町並み保存館
Saga Toriimoto Preservation District
鳥居本の町並み

Gosha-jinja Shrine
五社神社

Kyu Sagagosyo Daihonzan Daikaku-ji Temple
旧嵯峨御所 大本山大覚寺
Kangetsu-no-yube P100
観月の夕べ P100

Osawa Pond
大沢池

Daikaku-ji
大覚寺

Adashino Nenbutsu-ji Temple
化野念仏寺

Gohodo-benten-mae
護法堂弁天前

Arashiyama Takao Parkway
嵐山高雄パークウェイ

Daikaku-ji-michi
大覚寺道

To Hirosawa Pond
広沢池へ

雄へ
To Takao

Gio-ji Temple
祇王寺

Seiryo-ji Temple
(Saga Shaka-do Temple)
清凉寺
(嵯峨釈迦堂)

Kobuchi-cho
小渕町

Amida-do
阿弥陀堂

Daikaku-ji-mon-mae
大覚寺門前

Taho-to
多宝塔

Saga Shakado-mae
嵯峨釈迦堂前

Hosho-in Temple
宝筐院

Nison-in Temple
二尊院

Rakushisha
落柿舎

Saga-shogakko-mae
嵯峨小学校前

Shinmarutamachi-dori
新丸太町通

To Route No.162
国道162号へ

Hozu-kyo
保津峡へ

Jojakko-ji Temple
常寂光寺

Otsuka
おおつか P67

Saga Setogawa-cho
嵯峨瀬戸川町

Saga Arashiyama Sta.
嵯峨嵐山駅

To Uzumasa.
太秦へ

JR Sanin Line (Sagano Line)
JR山陰本線(嵯峨野線)
Ogura Tunnel
小倉トンネル

Chikurin-no michi
Ogura Pond
竹林の道 P36
小倉池

Nonomiya-jinja Shrine
野宮神社
P29·36

Sagano Romantic Train P37
嵯峨野トロッコ列車
Sagano Romantic Train P37

Torokko Saga Sta.
トロッコ嵯峨駅

Sagano Romantic Train (Torokko Train)
嵯峨野観光鉄道(トロッコ列車)

To Rokuo-in
鹿王院へ

Randen
Saga-eki Sta.
嵐電嵯峨駅

To Trokko
ロッコ保津峡へ

Arashiyama Tunnel
嵐山トンネル

Tenryu-ji Temple, Shigetsu
天龍寺 篩月

Burari Arashiyama
ぶらり嵐山

Arashiyama Sta.
Hannari Hokkori Square
嵐山駅はんなり・
ほっこりスクエア

Keifuku Ry.
Arashiyama Line
(Randen)

Arashiyama
Myoken-do
嵐山妙見堂

Okochi Sanso Garden
大河内山荘庭園 P37

Torokko
嵐山駅 P37
Torokko
Arashiyama
Sta.
トロッコ嵐山駅

Tenryu-ji Temple
天龍寺
P9·20·36
天龍寺庭園

京福嵐山線(嵐電)
Keifuku Arashiyama Line (Randen)

Daihikaku
(Senko-ji Temple)
大悲閣
(千光寺)

Sogen Pond
曹源池

(京都)
京都嵐山駅前
Keifuku Arashiyama-eki-mae
Kyoto-bus

Arashiyama Sta.
嵐山駅

To Hanazono
花園方面へ

Arashiyama Park
Kameyama-chiku
嵐山公園
亀山地区

Shigure-den
時雨殿

Hozugawa River
保津川

Togetsu-kyo
渡月橋

Arashiyama

Kiyotaki-michi Sanjo
清滝道三条

Hogon-in, sub-temple of Tenryu-ji Temple
天龍寺 宝厳院

Oigawa River
(Hozugawa River)
大堰川
保津川

Hozugawa River
Boat Ride
保津川下り P37
Boat Ride boat slip
保津川下り着船場 P37

Togetsu-kyo
渡月橋

Katsuragawa River
桂川 Katsuragawa River

Arashiyama Park Nakanoshima-chiku
嵐山公園中之島地区
Nakanoshima Koen (Kyoto) Arashiyama Koen
Kyoto-bus
中の島公園(京都)
Nakanoshima-bashi
中ノ島橋

Togetsu Kobashi
渡月小橋

Hankyu
Arashiyama Sta.
阪急嵐山駅

Arashiyama
Monkey Park
Iwatayama
嵐山モンキーパーク
いわたやま P38

岩田山公園
Iwatayama Park

Hankyu Arashiyama-eki-mae
阪急嵐山駅前

Arashiyama Hybrid Museum
嵐山ハイブリッド美術館

To
Matsuo
松尾へ

Hankyu Ry.
Arashiyama Line
阪急嵐山線

Kokuzo
Horin-ji Temple
虚空蔵
法輪寺

To Katsura
桂方面へ

Arashiyama
嵐山

N

0 — 200m

A

B

C

二条大橋 Nijo-ohashi Bridge
京都ホテルオークラ Kyoto Hotel Okura

Prefectural Library 府立図書館

National Museum of Modern Art
国立近代美術館

Okazaki Koen/
Bijutsukan,
Heian Jingu-mae
岡崎公園 美術館・
平安神宮前

琵琶湖疏水
Biwako-sosui

Kyoto Municipal Museum of Art
京都市美術館

Kyoto Shiyakusho-mae Sta.
京都市役所前駅

Oike-ohashi Bridge 御池大橋

Kyoto Royal
Hotel&Spa
京都ロイヤル
ホテル&スパ

Matsuhiro Shoten
まつひろ商店 P56

Kyoto Municipal Zoo
京都市動物園

1

Honno-ji
Temple
本能寺

Samurai Kembu Theater
サムライ剣舞シアター P42

Higashiyama Sta.
東山駅

Sanjo-ohashi Bridge
三条大橋

地下鉄東西線

Subway Tozai Line

Sanjo Keihan Sta.
三条京阪駅

Jingu-michi
神宮道

Sanjo Sta.
三条駅

Higashiyama Sanjo
東山三条

Shoren-in
Monzeki Temp
青蓮院門跡 P21

Ponto-cho Kaburen-jo
先斗町歌舞練場

Kyo Hayashiya
京はやしや P60

一澤信三郎帆布
Ichizawa Shinzaburo Hanpu

Chion-ir
Temple
知恩院

Kyoto Kakefuda
京都 掛札 P56

白川 Shirakawa River

Tatsumi Daimyojin Shrine
辰巳大明神 P50

2

Shirakawa-
Minami-dori Street
白川南通 P50

Choboya
いや（ちょばや）P57
Yoshimoto Gion
Kagetsu
よしもと祇園花月

Takasegawa River

Kamogawa River

高瀬川

鴨川

Saryo Tsujiri
茶寮都路里 P61

Gion
祇園

Gion Matsuri
祇園祭 P99

Maruyama Park P17
円山公園

Kawaramachi Sta.
河原町駅

Shijo-ohashi Bridge
四条大橋

Gion Sakai
ぎをん さかい P61

Yasaka-jinja
Shrine
八坂神社

Takashimaya
高島屋

• Marui
マルイ

河原町通

Minami-za
南座

四条通 Shijo-dori

Choraku
Temple
長楽寺

Gion Shijo Sta.
祇園四条駅

Tsujiri
辻利 P61

花見小路通界隈

Gion Kawakami
祇園川上 P63

Entoku-in,sub-temple of
Kodai-ji Temple
高台寺 圓徳院

3

Kawaramachi-dori

川原町通

Gion Corner
ギオン
コーナー P50

Kodai-ji Temple

Hatsu-Ebisu-
初えびす P101

Kennin-ji
Temple
建仁寺

Gion Kobu
Kaburen-jo
祇園甲部歌舞練場

高台寺 P21

Kyoto Ebisu-jinja Shrine
京都恵美須神社

Miyako-odori
都をどり P98

Kyoto Higashi-yama Hanatoro
京都・東山花灯路 P98

Miyagawa-cho
Beer Garden
宮川町ビアガーデン P50

Higashiyama Yasui
東山安井

Ten-qoo-ann
天空庵 P12

Ryozen Kannon
Temple
霊山観音

Yasui Konpira-gu Shrine
安井金比羅宮 P31

Minatoya
港屋 P12

Ryozen Museum of History
霊山歴史館

Kushi Matsuri P100
櫛まつり

Kiyomizu-
michi
清水道

Maiko Transformation Studio S
舞妓変身スタジオ 四季 P51

Rokudo Chinno-ji Temple
六道珍皇寺

Kongo-ji
Temple
(Yasaka-)
金剛寺
(八坂庚申堂)

Hokan-ji
Temple
(Yasaka-no-to)
法観寺(八坂塔)

Shoeido
松栄堂 P13

Rokuharamitsu-ji Temple
六波羅蜜寺

Joju-in, sub-temple
of Kiyomizu-dera Temple
清水寺 成就院

Kiyomizu Gojo Sta.
清水五条駅

Koshin-do Temple
八坂庚申堂

Shichimiya Honpo
七味家本舗

Jishu-jinja Shrine
地主神社 P30

4

Gojo-ohashi Bridge
五条大橋

五条通 Gojo-dori

Kyoto Kitayama Malebranche,
Kiyomizu-zaka shop
京都北山マールブランシュ 清水店 P61

N

Rakuchu
洛中拡大図

Gojo-zaka Toki Matsuri
五条坂陶器まつり P99

五条坂
Gojo-zaka

P8-10 清水寺

Kiyomizu-dera Temple

0   150m

A

B

C

㉝ Local tours in Kyoto

| 現地ツアー |

How to learn more
☆ もっと深く知るなら

Join a local tour once you've arrived at your intended location. You can join alone or as a group, and they are definitely recommended if this is your first time in Kyoto.

目的地に着いてから参加する現地ツアー。ひとりからでも参加でき、京都に来るのが初めての人にも安心だ。

SUNRISE TOUR

Sunrise offers a wide variety of tours from trying on *kimono*, sake-tasting, and experiencing the tea ceremony, to strolling in a bamboo forest or visiting temples and shrines. The most popular is the *Kyoto Ichinichi Kanko* (One-day Kyoto Trip; prices starting at 13,200yen), during which you'll visit such places as Nijo-jo Castle, Kinkaku-ji Temple and Kiyomizu-dera Temple.

着付け、日本酒試飲、茶道などの体験型から、竹林散策や寺社参拝まで幅広いツアーが充実しており、自分の趣旨に合わせて選べる。一番人気の京都1日観光は、二条城、金閣寺、清水寺などを巡る1万3200円～。

♪ JTB West, Sunrise Center
JTB西日本 サンライズセンター
☎075-341-1413
🚶⏱💴¥ Differs depending on the tour
Number of participants: Differs depending on the tour / Reservations: By Internet
http://www.jtb.co.jp/shop/itdw/info/e/

Kyoto Cycling Tour Project
京都サイクリングツアープロジェクト

Guided cycling tours will bring you not only to such tourist locations as Arashiyama and Nijo-jo Castle, but also down pleasant narrow side streets and the path along the Kamogawa River. One especially popular tour is the Back Street Tour, during which you visit the area around Miyagawa-cho and Gion, go along the Shirawawa River and also cycle around the neighborhood near the Kyoto Gyoen National Garden.

案内人付きサイクリングツアーでは、嵐山や二条城などの観光地だけではなく、細い路地や鴨川遊歩道の走行も魅力。宮川町・祇園界隈、白川沿いや、京都御苑界隈を巡る「京都ろじ裏散歩」は、人気が高い。

○ Kyoto Cycling Tour Project
京都サイクリングツアープロジェクト
☎075-354-3636
🚶⏱💴¥ Differs depending on the tour
Number of participants: One person or more
Reservations: Telephone, email, or Internet
http://www.kctp.net/en/

Walk in Kyoto Talk in English

In this tour, a knowledgeable guide will give you in-depth explanations and answers to your questions as you visit places not usually shown to the public to see how *juzu* prayer beads, *sensu* folding fans, *tatami* mats, pottery and other traditional handicrafts are made. During the tour, you'll be taking a break at a traditional Japanese confectionery shop to have a sweet with Japanese tea.

ベテランガイドが丁寧に説明し、疑問に答えるこのツアーは、数珠、扇子、畳、陶器などの、普段は公開していない伝統産業製品の制作過程を見学。老舗和菓子店でお菓子と日本茶の休憩がある。

○ WaRaiDo 和来堂
☎075-366-6238
💴¥ 2,000yen / Number of participants: Approx 30 per group/
⏱10:00-15:00 (On Mondays, Wednesdays and Fridays) Not held in winter (From Dec. to Feb.)
Reservations: resevation not required
http://www.waraido.com/walking/index.html

Kyoto Kanko Yoru-bus
(Kyoto Sightseeing Evening Bus)
京都観光よるバス

This evening bus tour lets you see aspects of Kyoto not visible during the daytime, allowing you to see World Heritage Sites and national-treasure buildings in a single tour, including the illuminated Heian-jingu Shrine and Chion-in Temple. Enjoy Kyoto's nighttime landscape through the windows of the bus.

昼間とは一味違った夜のバスツアーでは、ライトアップされた平安神宮や知恩院など世界遺産・国宝建築を一度に巡る。バスの窓越しから夜の京都市内を楽しむこともできる。

○ MK Travel MKトラベル
☎075-662-1700 / 🚶 Differs depending on the tour ⏱ Hours: One tour a day starting at 19:50, taking about 1 hour and 35 minutes. 💴¥ 1,600yen (Guidance in English available for an extra 500 yen) Tour days: Thursdays, Fridays, Saturdays and nights before holidays
Reservations: Telephone or Internet (Reservations are not required, but people with reservations will be given priority at busy times.)
https://www.mk-bus.com/bustour/yorubus.html (Japanese)

34 Attending workshops

| 体験観光 |

Symbol guide
- Has an English homepage
- OK Can correspond in English
- Has English-language pamphlets

Learn a new craft!

✿ 職人技に挑戦!

Here are some examples of places where visitors can get an understanding of the traditional manufacturing techniques that have continually evolved in Kyoto for 1,200 years. Watch the artisans at work, then receive instruction as you try your own hand at creating something.

1200年の歴史の中で磨かれてきた、日本を代表する京都の伝統産業のものづくりのプロセスを体験できる施設にご案内。熟練された職人の技術を目の前で見てから、手ほどきを受けながら自分も体験することができる。

4 Demonstration: You can watch demonstrations by craftsmen who are the backbone of the traditional industries. (Usually from 10:00 – 16:30)

4. 実演:伝統産業を支える職人による実演を見ることができる(通常10時~16時30分)

Yuzen-zome Kyoto Museum of Traditional Crafts

京都伝統産業ふれあい館

Many of the items on display have been designated as traditional Kyoto craftworks, and you can view them close up. There are also videos showing the processes and production techniques used from beginning to end in creating a product. If you want to gain deeper knowledge, guidance by the curator or introduction to the atelier is also available.
Visitors can try their hand at *surigata-yuzen* (stencil-dyeing) to make handkerchief (from 900yen), paper fan (1,200yen), T-shirt (2,000yen) or other item.
The dyeing workshop is held only on Sundays (reservation not required).

京都の伝統産業製品が多数展示され、間近に見ることができる。作品が完成するまでの過程や技術を映像で観ることもでき、深く知りたい人には館長がガイダンスや工房紹介もしてくれる。
「摺型友禅染め」の体験コーナーでは、ハンカチ900円~、うちわ1200円、Tシャツ2000円などを制作。毎週日曜のみ体験可(予約不要)。

☎075-762-2670 P75-F1 8 minute walk from Higashiyama Station on the Tozai subway line ¥ Free ⏱9:00 – 17:00 (Admission until 16:30) CL Dec. 29 to Jan. 3

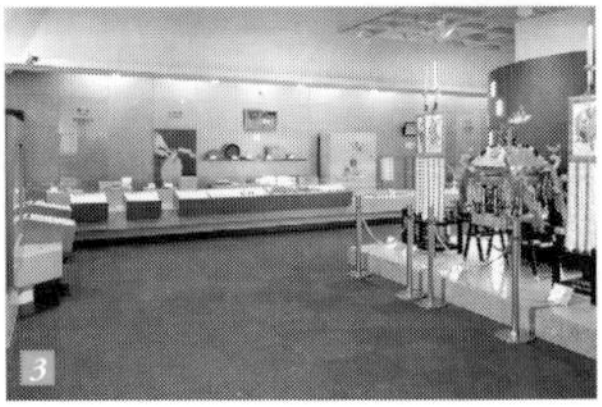

1 How to do surigata-yuzen: Place a paper pattern on a piece of fabric, then apply the dye to the fabric using a brush.
2 Permanent exhibition hall: Approximately 500 items representing 74 kinds of traditional Kyoto craftworks are regularly on display and for sale
3 Gallery: Displays fine arts and craftworks of important historical value

1. 摺型友禅染め体験:型紙を生地の上に置き、刷毛に染料を付けて摺り込んで染める
2. 常設展:京都の伝統産業製品74品目、約500点を常時展示・販売
3. ギャラリー:歴史的・資料的価値の高い美術・工芸品を展示

Nishijin Textile Nishijin Textile Center 西陣織会館

Watch the *kimono* show and hand weaving demonstration, then try both for yourself. (from 3,000yen to try *kimono*; 2,000yen for hand weaving)

着物ショーや手織り実演を見学。着付け（3000円〜）や手織り（2000円）の体験にも挑戦してみよう。

☎075-451-9231
📍P76-B3
🚶1 minute walk from the Kyoto City Bus Horikawa-imadega-wa bus stop
¥ Free
🕘9:00 – 17:00
📅Open year round 7 days a week

Shibori-zome Kyoto Shibori Museum 京都絞り工芸館

This is a popular workshop in which you dye a scarf using the silk-dyeing technique known as *"shibori-zome"*. It takes about one hour, and prices start at 3,000 yen.

絹の布を染める技術のひとつ「絞り染め」によるスカーフ染め体験が人気（所要時間約1時間、3000円〜）。

☎075-221-4252
📍P74-C2
🚶5 minute walk from Nijo-jo-mae Station on the Tozai subway line
¥ 500yen
🕘9:00 – 17:00
📅Unscheduled

Bamboo Yokoyama Bamboo Products 横山竹材店

This company makes various bamboo products. Try making your own chopsticks (for 4,000 yen) or a basket (3,500yen - 4,200yen).

「竹」で作った商品を製造販売。箸作り（4000円）や竹カゴ作り（3500〜4200円）体験ができる。

☎075-441-3981
📍P76-C4
🚶3 minute walk from the Kyoto City Bus Horikawa-shi-mochoja-machi bus stop
¥ Free 🕘9:00 – 17:00
📅Sundays and holidays

Japanese tea Marukyu Koyamaen, Makishima factory 丸久小山園 槇島工場

Visit this tea factory and take part in a tea ceremony. Enjoy some matcha and learn about sado etiquette.

抹茶工場見学や茶室体験、抹茶の試飲や作法の体験ができる。

☎0774-20-0909 (Reservation)
📍P71-C6
🚶About 5 minutes by taxi from Mukaijima Station on the Kintetsu line.
¥ 500yen
🕘10:00 – 12:00, 13:00 – 16:00
📅Sundays and holidays

sake Gekkeikan Okura Sake Museum 月桂冠大倉記念館

Learn the history of sake and the processes that go into making it by visiting a sake brewery. You will also have the opportunity to do tasting of ginjo-sake, which are available only at the museum, and plum wine.

酒蔵見学で日本酒造りの歴史やプロセスがわかる。記念館限定の吟醸酒やプラムワインを利き酒体験できる。
☎075-623-2056 📍P71-C5
🚶6 minute walk from Chusho-jima Station on the Keihan line ¥ 300yen (includes a gift) 🕘9:30 – 16:30
📅Open year round 7 days a week

Japanese doll Ando Ningyo-shop 安藤人形店

The family that operates this doll shop has been making Kyo-ningyo(Kyoto-style dolls) since the early 20th century. Visitors can see how they create various traditional dolls, and can even try

dressing up an *ichimatsu* doll that they can take home. (50,000 yen)

明治時代より続く京人形の老舗。雛人形・五月人形作りの見学や、市松人形への着付け体験（5万円。持ち帰り）ができる。

☎075-231-7466 📍P76-B4
🚶7 minute walk from Marutamachi Station on the Karasuma subway line
¥ Free 🕘9:00 – 18:00 📅Always open from Jan. 3 to May 2. During other periods, closed on Sundays and holidays

㉟ Manners & Etiquette

| マナーとエチケット |

Japanese manners to know
✿ 知っておきたい日本でのマナー

As is true in any country, Japan has its own form of etiquette. Learning and following the rules of etiquette when visiting various tourist spots or enjoying a meal will ensure you get a truly satisfying experience of Japanese culture.

世界各国にはそれぞれ常識や作法があるように、日本にも独自のマナーがある。観光地を訪れるときや食事の際など、マナーを知って守ることが、日本の文化をしっかり体験することにもつながる。

1 Avoid being noisy
騒がない、大声で話さない

People should always avoid making too much noise or speaking loudly in temples, shrines, restaurants, or on public transit. Using mobile phones is generally prohibited as well.

寺院や神社、レストラン、公共の交通機関では、大きな声で騒いだり話してはいけない。携帯電話も原則として通話は禁止である。

2 Get in the queue
列に並び、前の人から順番に

You should never cut in line when people are queued for a tourist attraction or for transportation. Go to the end of the line and patiently wait your turn.

観光地の見学や乗り物待ちで人が並んでいる場合、前の人を抜かしてはいけない。一番後ろに並び、自分の順番が来るまで静かに待とう。

3 Smoke in designated areas
喫煙は決められた場所で

Smoking is prohibited outside of designated smoking areas. Always deposit your cigarette butts in an ashtray.

決められた場所以外での喫煙は厳禁。吸殻は必ず灰皿に捨てること。

4 Take your garbage with you
ゴミは持ち帰る

Always take your garbage with you if you can't find the proper receptacle. When you do find one, make sure you sort your garbage into the proper bins.

ゴミ箱がない場所では、自分で出したゴミは持ち帰ること。また、ゴミの種類によって捨てる場所が分かれている場合は、該当するゴミ箱に捨てること。

5 Prohibited photography
撮影禁止

Please obey the signs that show when photography is prohibited. In addition, please do not bother the maiko *or* geiko with inappropriate photos or requests to have photos taken.

撮影禁止の注意書きがある文化財は絶対に撮ってはいけない。また、芸妓・舞妓さんなどに対してもみだりにカメラを向けたり、記念撮影を頼んではいけない。

6 Getting a taxi
タクシーの乗り方

If you want to take a taxi, wait at a taxi stand or hail a taxi on the street. Upon arriving at your destination, pay the fare before exiting. You don't need to pay a tip.

タクシーに乗りたい場合は、専用のタクシー乗り場で待つか走行中のタクシーに片手をあげ合図をし、停車させる。目的地に着いたら料金を支払って降りる。チップは不要。

7 Using a traditional toilet
和式トイレの使い方

Japanese-style toilet bowls are embedded in the floor. Squat down over the bowl facing frontward (toward the raised part of the bowl) when using one.

「和式トイレ」とは、床に便器が埋め込まれているスタイルのもので、前向きに便器をまたいで用を足す。

8 Chopstick manners
箸のマナー

Stabbing food with chopsticks is considered poor manners. Avoid resting your elbows on the table while eating.

食べ物に箸を突き刺すのはNG。食事中はひじをつかないようにする。

9 Taking off your shoes
家に入るときは靴を脱ぐ

In Japan, people remove their shoes at the entrance. Place your shoes with the toes pointed towards the door or place them in the shoe shelves if available.

日本では、玄関で靴を脱いで家に入る。脱いだ靴は、つま先側を外に向けて揃えておくとよい。靴箱がある場合は、中に入れる。

10 Communal bathing etiquette
大浴場に入る

Always wash your body with hot water when you enter a communal bathing area, and before you slip quietly into the bath. Swimming is not allowed in bathing areas. Also, never put your towel in the water or pull the plug in the tub.

大浴場に入ったら、まず湯をかけて身体を洗い清めてからバスタブに静かに入る。湯船の中で泳いではいけない。タオルを入れてはいけない。栓を抜かない。

36 Ryokan ｜旅館｜

Experience true hospitality
✿ おもてなし体験

From welcoming you upon your arrival to seeing you off as you depart, you will be catered to in the spirit of the uniquely Japanese hospitality that is rooted in this type of accommodation. Professional wait staff called *nakai* serve your food, prepare your *futon*, and attend to other needs during your stay. Dinner and breakfast are generally included in the price, and guests are free to move about the ryokan in a *yukata* and slippers.

日本独特のおもてなしの精神が根付いた宿泊施設で、出迎えから見送りまで行き届いた歓待がされる。「仲居」と呼ばれる専属の客室係が食事や布団の準備などさまざまな世話をしてくれる。食事は夕食・朝食の2食付きが基本。旅館内は浴衣姿・スリッパ履きでOK。

1 **Hospitality** **Check-in** チェックイン

After checking in at the front desk, the *nakai* will show you to your room. You will be served Japanese tea and sweets in the lobby or your room.

フロントでチェックインすると仲居さんが客室まで案内してくれる。ロビーまたは客室でお茶とお菓子のサービスがある。

For the finest in traditional Japanese hospitality
おもてなしの宿

Matsui Honkan 松井本館

This ryokan has been in business for 82 years and is conveniently located in the downtown area of Kyoto. You can enjoy authentic Kyoto-style cuisine at dinner. Free Wi-Fi is available throughout the building and in all of the guestrooms.

創業82年。京都の繁華街にありアクセスも便利。夕食は本格京料理。全館・全客室Wi-fi完備、無料で利用できる。

☎075-221-3535 ♥ P75-D2
🚶7 minute walk from Shijo Station on the Karasuma subway line ｜ Minimum 21,600yen per person for one night with dinner and breakfast (The rate differs depending on the season, day of week and room.) ⏰ Check in: 16:00 / Check out 10:00 ⊙ Open year round 7 days a week

2 **Hospitality** **Dinner** 夕食

Dinner is either served in your room or in a dining area. Beginning with the appetizer and ending with a dessert fruit, the *nakai* brings the food in predetermined order, sets the table and explains each dish. You can order drinks too.

客室（もしくは食事処）で食べる。料理は、先付から水菓子まで決まった順番で仲居さんが運んでくれ、セッティングや説明をしてくれる。飲み物の注文も可能。

3 Hospitality *Bathing* 大浴場

Guest rooms also have baths, but the communal bath is recommended as it is much larger and more open. You will find towels and a *yukata* to change into in your room.

風呂は客室にもあるが、大浴場のほうが湯船が広く解放感がありおすすめ。着替えの浴衣やタオルは、客室に備えてあるので大浴場に持参する。

4 Hospitality *Sleeping* 睡眠

A short while after dinner, *futons* are laid out for you in your room. Sleeping on a *futon* on straw *tatami* mat floors feels comfortable and spacious.

夕食後しばらくすると布団が敷かれる。畳の上に敷かれた布団で眠るのは心地よい。

5 Hospitality *Breakfast* 朝食

The breakfast menu generally includes freshly cooked rice, dried sheets of seaweed, grilled fish, Japanese soup and a personal hot pot. Some ryokan offer Western-style breakfasts as well.

朝食は炊きたての御飯、海苔、焼き魚、吸い物、小鍋などが出る。洋食を選べるところもある。

6 Hospitality *Seeing you off* お見送り

Once you have checked out, the *okami* (proprietress) and other staff will come outside to see you off.

チェックアウトが終わると、女将さんやスタッフが送ってくれる。

Some things to remember at a *ryokan*　旅館のNG

☑ No tipping is required.
チップは不要

☑ Pay for any drinks you take from the fridge.
冷蔵庫のドリンクは有料

✗ Don't take your *yukata* home with you.
浴衣の持ち帰り禁止

✗ Don't wear slippers on *tatami* mats.
畳の上をスリッパで歩かない

✗ Don't drag suitcase on the *tatami* mats.
畳の上でスーツケースを引きずらない

* Tatami mats are Japanese traditional floor material made of *igusa* (rushes) and are very delicate.
※日本の伝統的な床材である畳は、イグサという植物を使用していてとてもデリケートです。

37 Shukubo (Temple lodging) ｜宿坊｜

Daishin-in is located within the expansive temple grounds of Myoshin-ji Temple, with guestrooms facing the gardens.
妙心寺の大心院は広い境内の中にあり、庭を囲んで宿坊の部屋がある

Staying at a temple
☆お寺に泊まる

When visiting Kyoto, you might want to try staying in a shukubo, an accommodation facility built on the grounds of a temple. Depending on the shukubo, you might have the opportunity to see Buddhist statues close up, eat *shojin ryori* (traditional vegetarian cuisine) and attend a daily temple routine called "*otsutome,*" where you chant a Buddhist sutra and do *zazen* seated meditation early in the morning.

京都に来たならば、寺院に併設された宿泊施設"宿坊"に泊まるのもおすすめ。宿坊によっては仏像を間近に見ることができたり、精進料理を食べたり、毎朝早朝にお経を読んで坐禅をする「お勤め」と呼ばれる行事に参加することもできる。

Staying at Daishin-in!
大心院に泊まってみました！

🕐 *15:00 Check-in* チェックイン → ❶

Go into the entranceway and ring the bell to call someone. Make a reservation for *otsutome* when you check in.
玄関に入ったらベルを鳴らして人を呼びます。チェックイン時に「お勤め」の予約をします。

🕐 *15:20 Move to the room* 案内されて部屋へ → ❷

These are simple Japanese-style rooms, with neither toilet nor TV. In the winter, guests are provided with a *kotatsu* heated table.
シンプルな和室。部屋にトイレやテレビはありません。冬はこたつがあります。

🕐 *16:30 Going out for dinner* 夕食のため外出

The temple does not provide dinner, so guests must eat elsewhere, but don't forget the curfew.
夕食は付いていないので、外食になります。門限があるので注意。

🕐 *21:00 Bathing* 風呂に入る

Rooms are not equipped with bathing facilities, so guests bathe in the communal baths.
部屋には風呂が付いていないので大浴場に行きます。

There is often no one at the entrance reception area, so you need to ring a bell to call someone.
玄関の受付には人がいないことが多い、ベルなどで人を呼ぶ。

Rooms are separated by sliding doors with no locks. You are responsible for your own valuables.
鍵がなく襖で区切られた部屋。貴重品は自己管理。

Breakfast is *shojin ryori*, and includes rice, miso soup, sesame *tofu*, and various vegetable dishes.
朝食の精進料理。ごはん、味噌汁、胡麻豆腐、野菜料理の膳。

☑ Reservations required 必ず予約

You must make your reservation at least a day in advance, and the earlier you do so, the better. Going with someone who understands Japanese would also be helpful.

当日の申し込みは不可。早期の予約がベター。日本語のわかる同伴者がいるとなおよい。

☑ Bring your own necessities 洗面用具などは自分で

Bring your own toiletries, pajamas and other necessities. The bathing room is communal and shared with other lodgers.

風呂は他の宿泊者と共同。洗面用具やパジャマなども自分で準備。

☑ Be conscious of the time 時間を守る

Make sure to respect the curfew, and keep quiet during the night. Guests are recommended to get to bed early so they can take part in the otsutome in the morning.

門限を守り、夜は静かに過ごそう。早寝早起きして朝のお勤めに参加するのがおすすめ。

○ Daishin-in, sub-temple of Myoshin-ji Temple 妙心寺大心院

☎075-461-5714 📍P78-B3
🚶10 minute walk from Hanazono Station on the JR Sagano line
[¥] 5,000yen per person for one night with breakfast ⏱ Check in: 15:00 / Check out 10:00 ① Open year round 7 days a week

🕙 22:00 Bedtime 就寝

Lights are turned off at 22:00. You will have to put out your *futon* yourself. Turn off the lights in your own room, and enjoy a night of silence.

消灯は22時。布団は自分で敷きます。
部屋の電気を消して静かに就寝。おやすみなさい。

🕔 5:00 Rise and shine 起床

Get up early to participate in the *otsutome*.

お勤めに参加するので早起きします。

🕕 6:00 Otsutome in the morning 朝のお勤め

Enter the main hall and listen to the chief priest chant a sutra before the boddhisattva Kannon.

本堂に入り、観音菩薩の前で住職の読経を聞きます。

🕢 7:30 Shojin-ryori breakfast 精進料理の朝食 → 3

Breakfast features shojin ryori (→P64), a type of vegetarian cuisine originally eaten by ascetic monks. It's very healthy.

仏教の修行僧が食していた料理「精進料理」(→P64) が朝食。とてもヘルシーです。

🕙 10:00 Check-out チェックアウト

Tidy up the room before checking out. Thanks for a pleasant stay!

使用した部屋はきれいに整えてからチェックアウト。お世話になりました。

Stay at a World Cultural Heritage Site!
世界遺産に泊まろう！

Ninna-ji Temple, Omuro Kaikan
仁和寺 御室会館

The accommodations and training facility are located on the premises of Ninna-ji Temple (→P17) a World Cultural Heritage Site. Lodgers will have the special opportunity of attending the morning *otsutome* held in the Kondo Hall, a national treasure. Free Wi-Fi is available. You will be provided with *yukata*, towels and toiletries.

世界文化遺産・仁和寺(→P17)境内にある宿泊・研修施設。宿泊客は特別に国宝の金堂で行われる朝のお勤めにも参加できる。無料Wi-Fi利用可能。浴衣、タオル、洗面道具付き。

☎075-464-3664 📍P78-A2
🚶3 minute walk from the Kyoto City Bus Omuro-ninnaji bus stop [¥] 6,200yen per person for one night with breakfast / 9,800yen per person for one night with dinner and breakfast ⏱ Check-in: 16:00- / Check-out: 9:00 ⊛ Open year round 7 days a week

38 Guesthouses

| ゲストハウス |

Multicultural accommodations

☆ 異文化交流できる宿

Guesthouses are recommended if you are planning on a long stay. The prices are reasonable and there are opportunities to exchange travel information with other guests and the staff. There is a variety of guesthouses, including those run in traditional *Kyo-machiya* townhouses and some that are also part restaurant or bar.

長期滞在をするならゲストハウスに宿泊するのもおすすめ。価格が安いのはもちろん、他のゲストやスタッフとの情報交換の場としても利用できる。宿の形態は、伝統ある京町家を利用した宿や飲食店を併設した宿など多種多様。

Some guesthouses hold various fun events.
ゲストハウスによってはいろいろなイベントが用意されている

Facilities in a guesthouse ゲストハウスの設備

Japanese-style rooms have straw *tatami*-mat floors that you can directly sit or laze about on. You prepare your own *futon* when you get ready for bed, and you fold it back up as shown in the photo when you're not using it.
宿泊部屋：和室は、畳の床に直接座ったり寝転んだりできる。布団は眠るとき自分で敷き、使わないときは写真の様に畳む。

Depending on the guesthouse, these rooms may be Japanese-style or Western-style, but they are all Japanese-style in that you must remove your shoes before entering. They are excellent places to meet other travelers.
リビング・ダイニング：ゲストハウスによって和室と洋室に分かれるが、どちらも靴を脱いで過ごす日本式のスタイル。他の宿泊者との交流の場にもなる。

You can prepare your own meals here, but make sure to clean up afterwards. You can use the dishes, eating utensils and microwave oven, and some guesthouses provide you with seasonings and a communal refrigerator.
キッチン：食事の準備や後片付けなどは自分でする。食器、電子レンジも利用できる。ゲストハウスによっては調味料や冷蔵庫も共用で使用できる。

Guesthouses have communal shower rooms, but it's fun to try a sento (public bathhouse) if there's one nearby. Bring your own towel, soap and other necessary bathing items.
シャワー：共同のシャワールームがあるが、近くに銭湯と呼ばれる大浴場がある場合、そちらを利用するのも面白い。銭湯にはタオルや石鹸などを持参する。

Len　Len

> *We want this to be a place where travelers and locals can meet and communicate.*
> 旅人と地元の方々との交流の場にしてください。

Seven types of rooms are available, including shared rooms accommodating up to eight people and private rooms. There is also a café/bar on the premises.

8人部屋から個室まで7タイプの部屋がある。宿泊施設にカフェバーも併設されている。

☎075-361-1177 ♀P75-D4
🚶12 minute walk from Gojo Station on the Karasuma subway line
¥ Mixed male-female dormitory room: From 2,600 yen per person per night / Female-only dormitory room: From 3,000 yen per person per night / Private room: From 3,200 yen per person per night /
⏱Check in: 16:00-22:00 / Check out: 11:00　🗓Open year round 7 days a week　Reservations: Internet
http://backpackersjapan.co.jp/kyotohostel/en/

Kyoto Guesthouse Roujiya

ろうじ屋

> *This is a quiet residential area, but it's conveniently located with a train station nearby as well as an old shopping street and public bath. It's also a comfortable and safe place for females traveling alone.*
> 周りは静かな住宅街ですが、駅からは近く、昔ながらの商店街や銭湯もある便利な場所です。一人の女性でも安心です。

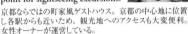

The proprieter of this guesthouse always makes sure that her guests enjoy their stay in this unique, Kyoto-style *machiya*. It is centrally located near a number of train and subway stations, making it a convenient starting point for sightseeing excursions.

京都ならではの町家風ゲストハウス。京都の中心地に位置し各駅からも近いため、観光地へのアクセスも大変便利。女性オーナーが運営している。

☎075-432-8494 ♀P74-B2
🚶6 minute walk from Nijo Station on the JR line
¥ Dormitory room: From 3,000 yen per person per night (There are both mixed male-female and female-only dormitory rooms) / *Tatami*-mat room: From 8,000 yen per room per night
⏱Check in: 16:00-22:00 / Check out: 10:00
🗓Open year round 7 days a week
Reservations: By telephone or Internet
http://kyotobase.com/

Rental bicycles: A bicycle is a very convenient way to get around Kyoto's many narrow roads. If your guesthouse doesn't provide them, go to your nearest bicycle rental shop.
レンタサイクル：京都は細い路地が多いので、自転車移動が大変便利。宿にレンタサイクルが無い場合は、近くのレンタサイクル店を利用しよう。

Pan and Circus

パンとサーカス

> *Young creative people from around the world gather here.*
> "世界中から集まる若き表現者たちのサロン"です。

A kyo-machiya more than 100 years old was renovated to create this guesthouse. Visitors can enjoy the antique furnishing and works by artists from around the globe in an eclectic marriage of East and West.

築100年以上の京町家を改装。世界各国アーティストの作品やアンティーク家具の和洋MIXで独特の雰囲気。

☎080-7085-0102 ♀P75-D4
🚶5 minute walk from Gojo Station on the Karasuma subway line
¥ Separate male or female dormitory room: 3,000 yen per person per night ⏱Check in: 15:00-21:00 / Check out: 11:00　🗓Open year round 7 days a week
Reservations: By telephone, Internet or email
http://panandcircus.com/en/

91

Kyoto Station Guide
京都駅ガイド

Take advantage of the many facilities available at Kyoto Station that will make your trip more comfortable.

京都駅には旅をより快適にする施設がたくさんあるので賢く利用しよう。

CHECK!
1) Get tourism, traffic and other travel information
2) Visit some of Kyoto's popular shops and restaurants
3) See the wide array of Kyoto souvenirs available

1) 観光情報や交通アクセスなど旅情報をゲットできる
2) 京都の人気グルメや名店が集まる
3) みやげが豊富に揃う

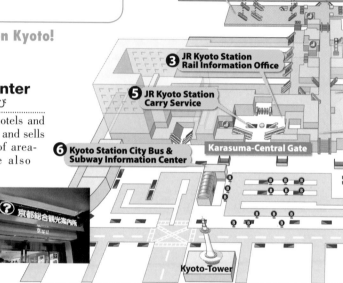

④ Kyoto Shinkansen Station Delivery Service

Hachijo-Gate

③ JR Kyoto Station Rail Information Office

⑤ JR Kyoto Station Carry Service

⑥ Kyoto Station City Bus & Subway Information Center

Karasuma-Central Gate

Kyoto-Tower

Get the latest info on Kyoto!
京都の最新情報をゲットしよう！

❶ Kyoto Tourist Information Center
京都総合観光案内所　京なび

Offers up-to-date info on hotels and other places around Kyoto, and sells event tickets. A variety of area-specific pamphlets are also available.

京都各地のタイムリーな情報提供や、宿泊案内、イベントのチケット販売を行う。各所のパンフレットも多数取り揃える。

☎ 075-343-0548
🕐 8:30-19:00
📅 Open year round

Come here for Kyoto Station Building info!
駅ビルのことなら何でもおまかせ

❷ Kyoto Station Building Information Center
京都駅ビル　インフォメーション

Provides help navigating the complex layout of Kyoto Station Building. An important resource of everything from station maps to cards providing directions to tourist spots.

複雑に入り組む京都駅ビルを案内。ビル内のマップや、観光地への交通案内カードなど重宝するアイテムが手に入る。

☎ 075-361-4401
🕐 10:00-19:00
📅 Open year round

The spot for Kyoto railway info
京都の鉄道アクセス案内はコチラ

❸ JR Kyoto Station Rail Information Office
JR 京都駅　鉄道案内所

Come here for easy-to-understand info on how to travel by rail. Particularly convenient for those travelling outside of the city center to places like Uji and Fushimi.

鉄道アクセスについて、分かりやすく情報を教えてくれる。特に宇治や伏見など、郊外へ出る際に利用すると便利。

☎ None
🕐 8:00-20:00
📅 Open year round

Drop off your heavy luggage and enjoy your day!
重たい荷物は預けて手ぶらで GO!

So you want to head off to the tourist spots, but you have a bunch of heavy luggage? If that's the case, why not use the Luggage Check Service? You can drop your bags off for pick-up later, or even have them forwarded to your hotel, so you can better enjoy your day!

すぐに目的地に向かいたいけど重い荷物は邪魔！という時は手荷物預かりサービスへ。一時預かりはもちろん、宿泊先への配達もしてくれるので、身軽に旅を楽しむことができる。

Tokaido Shinkansen

1 Kyoto Tourist Information Center

2 Kyoto Station Building Information Center

Post Office

Symbol guide
🚆 JR Ticket Resevation Office
🅱 Bus Stop

Hachijo Exit East Side 八条口東側

4 Kyoto Shinkansen Station Delivery Service
新幹線京都駅 デリバリーサービス

☎075-671-8026 ● 750 yen/item
⏱9:00-20:00 (Check open until 14:00)
CL Open year round
http://delivery-service.jp/

Karasuma Central Exit Basement
烏丸中央口地下

5 JR Kyoto Station Carry Service
JR 京都駅 キャリーサービス

☎075-352-5437
● 750 yen/item
⏱8:00-20:00
(Check open until 14:00)
CL Open year round
http://carry-s.com/

Get a route map
路線マップが手に入る

6 Kyoto Station City Bus & Subway Information Center
京都駅前 市バス・地下鉄案内所

City Bus & Subway Information Center is located outside Kyoto Station Karasuma Central Exit to the right. Many deals available, including a Day Ticket for unlimited travel on City Bus and Kyoto Bus (certain areas excluded). Get City Bus route map when you buy tickets here.

京都駅の烏丸中央口改札を出て右手にある、市バスと地下鉄の案内所。市バスと京都バスが乗り放題（一部区間を除く）になる市バス・京都バス一日乗車券などお得なチケットの販売も。乗車券を購入すると市バスの路線マップをもらえる。

☎075-371-4474 ⏱7:30-19:30 CL Open year round

Bus Guide Quick Facts
バス早わかりガイド

Buses are a convenient way to get around the tourist spots, but with so many bus routes to choose from, it can be hard to find the right bus. First thing's first – make your way to City Bus/Subway Information Center.

観光スポットをまわるのは、バスでの移動が便利。しかし、路線数が多く、すべてを理解するのはとても難しい。まずは京都駅前市バス・地下鉄案内所（➡P93）へ立ち寄ろう。

Kyoto Station Bus Terminal
京都駅のバスターミナル

Located just outside Karasuma Central Exit with stops for Kyoto City Buses, Kyoto Bus, JR Bus, Keihan Bus, and other companies.

烏丸中央口前にある。市バス・京都バス・西日本JRバス・京阪バスなどのバスが発着する。

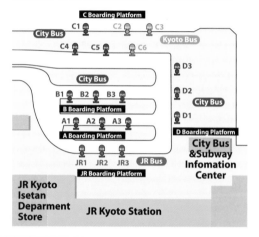

Three bus operators - all you need to know
3つのバス会社をCHECK!

Great for getting around town
市街地の移動に便利

City Bus
市バス

City Bus operates 75 routes in the city from downtown to the suburbs. Most lines cost a flat fare of 230 yen, including Raku Bus (➡P95), but buses going to the suburbs operate on a ticket-based system, and fares depend on where you get on the bus.

市街地を中心に郊外まで、75の路線を運行。洛バス（➡P95）も含め多くの路線が230円均一の後払いだが、郊外へ出る路線は整理券方式で、乗車区間により運賃が異なる。

Heading for Arashiyama or Ohara
嵐山・大原方面に便利

Kyoto Bus
京都バス

Operates from Kyoto Station, Sanjo-Keihan, Demachiyanagi Station, and Kokusaikaikan Station towards Uzumasa, Arashiyama, Ohara, Kurama and Kibune.

京都駅・三条京阪・出町柳駅・国際会館駅などから太秦・嵐山方面や大原・貴船・鞍馬方面へ運行。

Heading for Takao or Shuzan
高雄・周山方面に便利

West JR Bus
西日本JRバス

Connects Kyoto Station with Takao and Shuzan by way of Kitano and Ryoan Temple, but be careful when boarding as half of the buses do not pass Ryoan Temple. Pick up a Takao Free Ticket at Kyoto Station and you can get on and off the bus whenever you like between Daishogun and Toganoo.

京都駅から北野・竜安寺前を経由し高雄・周山を結ぶ。ただし半数は竜安寺前を通らないので注意。京都駅から「高雄フリー乗車券」（800円）を使えば大将軍～栂ノ尾間は乗り降り自由。

Raku Bus – Perfect for Tourists

観光にとっても便利な「洛バス」

Express city bus service connecting famous tourist spots. Set fare of 230 yen, but can be boarded by holders of a Kyoto Sightseeing One-day Pass or Kyoto City Bus & Kyoto Bus One-Day Pass. There are three routes and the buses are color-coded to match: **peach for Route 100, green for 101, and yellow for 102.** See the map below or info on routes and tourist spots.

市バスが運行する観光名所を結ぶ急行便。運賃は230円均一。「京都観光一日乗車券」「市バス・京都バス一日乗車券カード」も利用可能。3系統あり、**100号系統は桃色、101号系統は緑、102号系統は黄色**のラッピング車両が目印だ。それぞれのルートや観光スポットは下図参照。

Raku Bus 100 Route

洛バス100号系統 桃色

For Higashi-yama, Heian Shrine, Ginkaku-ji peach

東山、平安神宮、銀閣寺方面

Raku Bus 101 Route

洛バス101号系統 緑

For Nijo Castle, Kitano Tenmangu, Kinkaku-ji green

二条城、北野天満宮、金閣寺方面

Raku Bus 102 Route

洛バス102号系統 黄色

For Kinkaku-ji, Daitoku-ji, Ginkaku-ji yellow

金閣寺、大徳寺、銀閣寺方面

Raku Bus Route Map 洛バス路線図

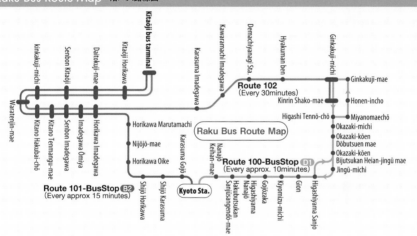

Using apps and websites to get around

便利なアプリやサイトを利用してスイスイ移動

Smartphone app shows when buses will arrive!

到着時刻もわかるスマホアプリ！

Free 無料

Arukumachi Kyoto
(Bus and Train Veteran)

歩くまち京都 (バス・鉄道の達人)

This app provides info on routes and transfers needed to get where you're going. Searchable by bus stops or tourist spots.

目的地までの経路などを調べられる乗換案内アプリ。バス停だけでなく観光名所からも検索可。

Get info on connections between a number of routes.

複数系統のバス接近状況がわかる

Free 無料

Pokeroke
ポケロケ

Select bus stop, bus route, or destination and get all the route connection information you need.

バス停留所・バス系統・行き先を選択すると、全系統のバス接近情報がわかるサイト。

Convenient and Reasonable Card

お得な乗車券

If you're planning on travelling to different spots around the city, it's best to pick up a one-day unlimited pass or one of the other special passes available.
You can buy these tickets at any city bus and subway information office or ticket office.

あちこち観光するなら、乗り降り自由の一日乗車券などを利用するのが断然お得。
京都駅前市バス・地下鉄案内所などで購入できる。

		City Bus/Kyoto Bus One Day Pass 市バス・京都バス 一日乗車券カード	Kyoto Tourism One-Day Pass 京都観光一日乗車券	Eigamura Excursion Pass - Eigamura/Arashiyama-Sagano 映画村入村券つき 映画村・嵐山嵯峨野回遊乗車券
Ticket Name チケット名				
Price 値段		500yen	1200yen	2400yen
Applicable trains/ buses 乗れる電車・バス	**Subway** 地下鉄	×	○	×
	City Bus 市バス	△※1	○	×
	Kyoto Bus 京都バス	△※1	△※2	△※3
Advice アドバイス		Less than 3 rides in the City Bus/Kyoto Bus flat fare area! Unlimited rides within the City Bus / Kyoto Bus 230yen flat fare area 市街地均一区間の市バス・京都バス3回でモト取り！ 市バス・京都バスの市内230円均一区間内が1日乗り放題	City + Arashiyama & Ohara: Less than 3 bus tickets + 3 basic subway fares! 1 ticket covers the main tourist attractions! Only 2000yen for 2 days! 市街地＋嵐山・大原：バス3回＋地下鉄初乗り3回でモト取り！おもな観光地はこれ1枚でOK。2日用は2000円	Eigamura + Arashiyama: Save on the trip to Eigamura and the entry ticket! Bus ticket is valid for 1 day, but only one entry to Eigamura possible. 映画村＋嵐山：映画村入村＋1回乗車でモト取り！京都バスの嵐山方面系統が1日乗り放題。映画村入村は1回限り
Contact 問合先		Kyoto Municipal Transportation Bureau City Bus Subway Information Center 京都市交通局 市バス・地下鉄案内所 ☎075-863-5200		Kyoto Bus 京都バス ☎075-871-7521

* 1) Only valid in the City Bus/Kyoto Bus 230yen flat fare area.
* 2) Valid on designated routes to Ohara and Iwakura in addition to the 230yen flat fare area.
* 3) Unlimited rides between Kyoto Bus point of departure and Arashiyama.
△※1)＝市バス・京都バスの市内230円均一区間のみ利用できる。
△※2)＝市内230円均一区間のほか、大原・岩倉方面の指定区間に乗車できる。
△※3)＝京都バスの京都駅前・三条京阪前・四条河原町～嵐山方面が1日乗り放題。

Deciphering City Bus destination signs, riding carefree

市バスの行き先表示を読み解いて、迷わず乗車

Look up route number, destination, or Line color!

系統番号と行き先、ラインカラーをチェック！

Start by confirming route number and destination. But be careful not to get on a bus going in the wrong direction on the circular routes. Also, Kyoto Bus operates buses in the same areas with the same route numbers, including 17, 71, 75, 84, so it's easy to get on the wrong bus (the routes themselves are completely different.) Bus colors show the route they take, so you can use that to choose a bus to avoid the worst traffic.

まずは系統番号と行き先を確認。循環系統は逆回りに乗らないよう要注意。また、17・71・75・84番などは同じエリアを走る京都バスにも同番号があり、乗り間違えやすい（路線は全く別）。ラインカラーはバスが走る通りが分かり、渋滞した道を避けるのに便利。

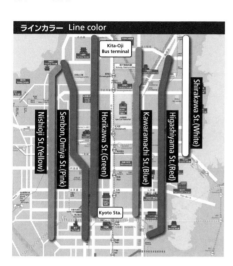

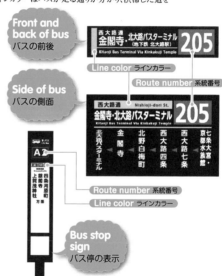

Front and back of bus
バスの前後

Side of bus
バスの側面

Bus stop sign
バス停の表示

Line color ラインカラー

Route number 系統番号

Route number 系統番号

Line color ラインカラー

Check anything Train

各電車の特徴

City Subway (Kyoto Municipal Transportation Bureau)

市営地下鉄（京都市交通局）

The Karasuma Line and Tozai Line cross at Karasuma Oike Station.

烏丸線と東西線の2路線。2路線がクロスするのは烏丸御池駅。

JR Sagano Line (Sanin Main Line)

JR嵯峨野線（山陰本線）

Provides a quick ride from Kyoto Station to Arashiyama. Catch the Torokko train for Hozu Gorge just outside Saga-Arashiyama Station.

京都駅から嵐山方面へは早くておすすめ。保津峡観光のトロッコ列車は嵯峨嵐山駅前から発車。

Randen (Keifuku Electric Railroad Arashiyama Line)

嵐電（京福電鉄嵐山線）

Connects Shijo-Omiya Station and Kitano Hakubaicho Station with the Sagano/Arashiyama area. Flat fare of 210 yen.

四条大宮・北野白梅町の両駅を起点に嵯峨野・嵐山方面を結ぶ。運賃は210円均一。

Keihan Main Line & Oto Line

京阪電鉄本線・鴨東線

Underground trains running along the Kamo River. Get off at the last stop, Demachiyanagi Station, to transfer to the Eizan Electric Railway to Kurama and Enryaku-ji Temple.

鴨川沿いの地下を走る。終点の出町柳駅で鞍馬・比叡山方面への叡山電鉄に接続。

Spring ＊春＊

March ·3月·

3   3日

Nagashi-bina
流し雛

Shimogamo-jinja shrine ◎下鴨神社

Dolls made with Japanese paper are floated down the mitarashi-gawa at the shrine as a way to pray for children to grow up healthy. Shrine visitors may also take part.

和紙で出来た人形を境内の御手洗川に流し、子どもの健やかな成長を願う行事。参拝者も参加できる。

Early to mid-month   上～中旬

Kyoto Higashi-yama Hanatoro 京都・東山花灯路

In the Higashiyama area ◎東山地域一帯

Ikebana and lanterns made of paper and bamboo decorate the stone paved path the runs from Shoren-in to Kiyomizu-dera. This early spring festival is a seasonal tradition that features a variety of different events.

青蓮院から清水寺までの石畳の道沿いを、和紙や竹で作った露地行灯の灯りと生け花が彩る。さまざまな企画が実施される。

April ·4月·

1～30   1～30日

Miyako-odori
都をどり

Gion-kobu Kaburen-jo ◎祇園甲部歌舞練場他

A festival of song and dance performed by geiko and maiko. The festival is held in April in three of Kyoto's five kagai geisha districts (except Gion-Higashibu and Ponto-cho).

芸妓・舞妓による踊りと唄の披露。京都に５つある「花街」（祇園甲部、祇園東、宮川町、先斗町、上七軒）のうち祇園東・先斗町以外の３花街では４月に行われる。

29   29日

Kyokusui no Utage
曲水の宴

Jonan-gu ◎城南宮

A reproduction of a pastime popular among the aristocracy in the Heian period. A cup is gently placed to float on the surface of a meandering river in a garden. Poets sit beside the river composing prose until their cup floats up for them to drink.

平安貴族の歌遊びを再現した行事。ゆるく曲がった小川の側に歌人が座り、小川に流される杯を受け取るまでに短歌を詠む。

May ·5月·

5   5日

Kamo-kurabe-uma
賀茂競馬

Kamigamo-jinja shrine ◎上賀茂神社

This ceremony has been held since 1093. Ceremonial-rider in traditional costume race against each other atop their horses.

競馬は「くらべうま」と読む。1093 年より続く行事で、騎手は古典的な衣装を身にまとい、馬場を駆け抜ける勝負を競う。

15   15日

Aoi Matsuri 葵祭
Kyoto Imperial Palace to Shimogamo-jinja shrine to Kamigamo-jinja shrine

◎京都御所～下鴨神社～上賀茂神社

Five hundred people in Heian period costumer walk about eight kilometers during this festival. People in the procession decorate themselves with leaves of the aoi plant.

平安王朝の衣装をまとった 500 人が約 8km にわたる道を行列する祭り。行列の参加者は葵の葉を身に着ける。

▲ High temp 最高気温：14.8℃
▼ Low temp 最低気温：4.9℃

⇧ Precipitation 降水量：
159.0mm

▲ High temp 最高気温：20.5℃
▼ Low temp 最低気温：10.9℃

⇧ Precipitation 降水量：
163.5mm

▲ High temp 最高気温：27.7℃
▼ Low temp 最低気温：15.8℃

⇧ Precipitation 降水量：
128.0mm

＊ The data on monthly average temperature high/low and monthly rainfall in Kyoto is taken from the website of the Japan Meteorological Agency. ＊ 2015 年の京都の月平均最高、最低気温と月合計降水量（気象庁 HP より）

Summer *·夏·*

June ·6月·

Mid-June to late September
中旬〜9月下旬

Ukai
鵜飼い

Ujigawa river ◎宇治川

Cormorants have been used for fishing on the Uji-gawa since ancient times. Beacon fires are lit, and traditional clothing is worn by participants.(Dates change each year.)

川で飼い慣らした鵜に魚を捕まえさせるのは、宇治川で行われてきた古来の漁法。かがり火を焚き、伝統的な装束で行う。（年により日程が異なる。）

・・・・・・・・・・・・・・・・・・・・

30   30日

Nagoshi no Harae 夏越祓
At various shrines in the city (Kifune-jinja shrine in photo)
◎市内各神社

Shrine visitors pass through a ring made of cogon grass to purify themselves of the previous six months of sins and transgressions, and to pray for the remaining six months to pass in good health.

境内に置かれた茅草で作った「茅の輪」をくぐり、半年分の罪や穢れを祓い、残り半年の無病息災を祈る行事。

July ·7月·

1〜31   1〜31日

Gion Matsuri
祇園祭

Kyoto City Center ◎市内中心部

Kyoto's biggest festival last's an entire month. Highlights includes the parades on the 17th and 24th, in which floats, called yamahoko in Kyoto, are carried along the parade route.

1カ月にわたる京都最大の祭り。ハイライトは17日と24日、山鉾とよばれる祭り用屋台が巡行する。

・・・・・・・・・・・・・・・・・・・・

Last five days of the month
下旬の五日間

Mitarashi-sai
御手洗祭

Shimogamo-jinja shrine ◎下鴨神社

Participants soak their feet in Mitarashi Pond in this ritual designed to give people an escape from the heat of summer and pray for good health. The votive candles at the water's edge lend the event a dream-like atmosphere.

御手洗池に足を浸し、蒸し暑い夏を健康に乗り切れるよう祈る行事。水辺に奉納するロウソクの灯りが幻想的。

August ·8月·

7〜10   7〜10日

Gojo-zaka Toki Matsuri
五条坂陶器まつり

Gojo-zaka ◎五条坂

Kyoto is home to the porcelain types known as kyo-yaki and kiyomizu-yaki, and this pottery festival features around 350 stalls selling Kyoto porcelain and ceramic pieces made in kilns around the country. One of the biggest pottery markets in Japan.

京都の京焼・清水焼を中心に全国各地の窯からおよそ350軒の露店が並ぶ。全国から集まる陶器市としては最大級の規模。

・・・・・・・・・・・・・・・・・・・・

16   16日

Gozan no Okuribi
五山送り火
Higashi-yama, Kita-yama, Nishi-yama
◎東山、北山、西山

The spirits of people's ancestors return to Earth during O-bon, and this ritual is conducted to send them back from where they came. Torches are used to form large Chinese characters and other pictures on five mountains.

お盆の期間に帰ってきた先祖の霊が、あの世に戻るのを見送る行事。5つの山に描かれた「大」などの文字や絵に火を灯す。

▲ High temp 最高気温：27.5℃
▼ Low temp 最低気温：18.9℃
☂ Precipitation 降水量：263.0mm

▲ High temp 最高気温：31.7℃
▼ Low temp 最低気温：23.8℃
☂ Precipitation 降水量：416.5mm

▲ High temp 最高気温：33.6℃
▼ Low temp 最低気温：24.6℃
☂ Precipitation 降水量：241.5mm

Autumn ＊秋＊

September ・9月・

September to October
9～10月

Kangetsu no yube
観月の夕べ

Daikaku-ji temple ◎大覚寺

Moon-viewing in September has long been a custom in Japan. Enjoy the Moon's beauty from a boat floating atop the pond called Osawa-no-ike, a popular moon-viewing spot since ancient times.

日本では9月の満月を愛でる習慣がある。古くから観月の名所であった大沢池に船を浮かべ満月を観賞する。

4th Monday 第4月曜日

Kushi Matsuri
櫛まつり

Yasui konpira-gu shrine
◎安井金比羅宮

A festival dedicated to appreciation of the common comb. A parade of women appear in hairstyles, makeup, and clothing ranging from the late 3rd century to the modern day.

日頃、愛用している櫛に感謝する祭り。古墳時代から現代まで、各時代の結髪と化粧、着物姿で行列する。

October ・10月・

22
22日

Jidai Matsuri 時代祭
Kyoto Imperial Palace to Heian-jingu shrine
◎京都御所～平安神宮

The "Festival of the Ages" features 2000 participants walking through the city in a variety of gorgeous reproductions of clothing from different eras. From that worn by the aristocracy in the 9th century to the clothing of 19th century Meiji Restoration ear political activists.

平安貴族から明治維新の志士まで、各時代の装束を再現した豪華絢爛な衣装を着た2000人の行列が市内を歩く。

22
22日

Kurama-no-hi Matsuri
鞍馬の火祭

Yuki-jinja shrine ◎由岐神社

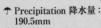

A famously eccentric festival. young peaple carry torches five meters tall, and walk the streets, calling out in loud voices as sparks scatter in the streets.

奇祭として有名。若衆たちが5メートルの火のついた松明を担ぎ、掛け声と共に火の粉を撒きながら練り歩く。

November ・11月・

October 30 ～ November 3
10月30日前後～11月3日前後

Aki-no-furuhon Matsuri
秋の古本まつり

Hyakumanben Chion-ji temple
◎百万遍知恩寺

A used book fair with around 200,000 books. Book auctions are also held. A number of books on the culture of Kyoto and Japan in general, both illustrated and otherwise.

約20万冊が販売され、オークションも開催されるイベント。京都や日本文化に関する書籍やビジュアル本も多い。

8
8日

Hitaki-sai
火焚祭

Fushimi Inari Taisha shrine
◎伏見稲荷大社

Tens of thousands of prayer sticks gathered from around Japan are burned in bonfires in appreciation of the abundant harvest, to purify one's transgressions and reduce obstacles, and to pray for one health and happiness.

全国から奉納された数十万本の願い事が書かれた火焚串を焚き、五穀豊饒に感謝し、罪やけがれの消滅、万福招来を祈る。

- ▲ High temp 最高気温：27.5℃
- ▼ Low temp 最低気温：19.5℃
- ⇑ Precipitation 降水量：190.5mm

- ▲ High temp 最高気温：23.9℃
- ▼ Low temp 最低気温：13.3℃
- ⇑ Precipitation 降水量：38.5mm

- ▲ High temp 最高気温：18.4℃
- ▼ Low temp 最低気温：11.2℃
- ⇑ Precipitation 降水量：177.0mm

＊ The data on monthly average temperature high/low and monthly rainfall in Kyoto is taken from the website of the Japan Meteorological Agency. ＊ 2015年の京都の月平均最高、最低気温と月合計降水量（気象庁HPより）

Winter * 冬 *

December · 12月 ·

21   21日

Shimai Kobo
終い弘法

Toji temple ◎東寺

The temple holds a market on the 21st of every month where people can buy curiosities and food. The final market of the year is the busiest, with stall-holders also selling food and decorations for the New Year celebrations.

毎月21日に行われる骨董店や飲食店などが並ぶ市。1年最後のこの日は正月用の食品や飾りも販売され最も賑わう。

31   31日

Joya-no-kane
除夜の鐘

Areas throughout the city ◎市内各所

Joya-no-kane is the custom of ringing temple bells 108 times on New Year's Eve through to New Year's Day. The ringing is said to free people from the 108 worldly desires. Some temples allow visitors to ring the bells.

大晦日の夜から元旦にかけて108回鳴らされるお寺の鐘のこと。鐘の音で人間のもつ108の煩悩を祓うと言われている。鐘を撞かせてくれる寺もある。

January · 1月 ·

1～3   1～3日

Hatsumode
初詣

Areas throughout the city ◎市内各所

A custom in which people visit shrines and temples at the beginning of the New Year in order to pray for a safe, healthy year. The approach roads and temple and shrine grounds are always packed with visitors.

新年のはじめに寺社を参詣し、一年の健康と安全を祈願する。多くの人が参拝し、参道も境内も賑わう。

8～12   8～12日

Hatsu-Ebisu
初ゑびす

Kyoto Ebisu-jinja shrine ◎京都恵美須神社

A New Year festival dedicated to Ebisu, the god of farming, commerce and fishing. Good luck charms are sold, and more than 1 million people visit every year in order to pray for a successful business year.

新年に行われる農業、商売、漁業の神・ゑびす神の祭り。縁起物も授与され、毎年100万人以上の人が商売繁盛を祈願に訪れる。

February · 2月 ·

2～4   2～4日

Setsubun Matsuri
節分祭

Yoshida-jinja shrine ◎吉田神社

A festival to ward off evil. A ceremony is conducted in which a god with a shield and spear chases away a raging demon. The approach road and surrounding area becomes home to more than 800 stalls.

邪気を祓う祭り。盾と矛を持った神様が、暴れる鬼を追い払う儀式がある。参道や周辺には800以上の露店が立つ。

25   25日

Baika-sai
梅花祭

Kitano Tenman-gu shrine ◎北野天満宮

The Plum Blossom is dedicated to this shrine's god of learning, Sugawara no Michizane, and is held in February to commemorate his death. There are around 1,500 plum trees of 50 different types in the garden for visitors to appreciate when their flowers bloom.

学問の神様である御祭神・菅原道真公の祥月命日に行われる祭典。梅苑が公開され、約50種1500本の梅が楽しめる。

▲ High temp 最高気温：13.2℃	
▼ Low temp 最低気温：5.3℃	
☂ Precipitation 降水量：101.0mm	

▲ High temp 最高気温：8.4℃
▼ Low temp 最低気温：2.2℃
☂ Precipitation 降水量：120.5mm

▲ High temp 最高気温：9.9℃
▼ Low temp 最低気温：2.3℃
☂ Precipitation 降水量：43.5mm

Conversation
日常会話 Nichijō kaiwa

Hello ハロー こんにちは ***konnichiwa***	**Goodbye** グッドバイ さようなら ***sayōnara***

Thank you. サンキュー ありがとう ***arigatō***	**You're welcome.** ユーアー ウェルカム どういたしまして ***dō itashimashite***	**Nice to meet you.** ナイス トゥ ミート ユー はじめまして ***hajimemashite***	**Yes No** イエス ノー はい いいえ ***hai iie***
Good morning グッド モーニング おはよう ***ohayō***	**Good evening** グッド イヴニング こんばんは ***konbanwa***	**Good night** グッド ナイト おやすみなさい ***oyasuminasai***	**See you.** スィー ユー じゃあ またね ***jaa ne***
I see. アイ スィ わかりました ***wakarimashita***	**I don't understand.** アイ ドント アンダースタンド わかりません ***wakarimasen***	**Excuse me.** エクスキューズ ミー すみません ***sumimasen***	**I am sorry.** アイアム ソーリー ごめんなさい ***gomen nasai***
Please プリーズ どうぞ ***dōzo***	**right?** ライト でしょ? ***desho***	**That's right!** ダッツ ライト その通り! ***sonotōri***	**You see,** ユー スィー あのね、 ***anone***
I must be going. アイ マスト ビー ゴーイング 失礼します ***shitsurei shimasu***	**No,thank you.** ノー サンキュー 結構です ***kekkō desu***	**May I help you?** メイ アイ ヘルプ ユー お手伝いしましょうか? ***otetsudai shimashō ka***	

What do you want to do? ワット ドゥ ユー ウォント トゥ ドゥ どうする? ***dōsuru***	**What's the date?** ホァッツ ダ デイト 今日は何月何日ですか? ***kyō wa nangatsu nan-nichi desuka***
What day is today? ホァット デイ イズ トゥデイ 今日は何曜日ですか? ***kyō wa nanyō bi desu ka***	**What time is it now?** ホァット タイム イズ イット ナウ 今、何時ですか? ***ima nanji desu ka***
How old are you? ハウ オールド アー ユー あなたはいくつですか? ***anata wa ikutsu desuka***	**Where are you from ?** ウエア アー ユー フロム どこから来ましたか? ***doko kara kimashita ka***
What do you do? ホァット ドゥ ユー ドゥ 仕事は何ですか? ***shigoto wa nan desu ka***	**When is your birthday?** ホェン イズ ユア バースデー あなたの誕生日はいつですか? ***anata no tanjōbi wa itsu desu ka***

one ワン 1 ***ichi***	**two** トゥー 2 ***ni***	**three** スリー 3 ***san***	**four** フォー 4 ***shi/yon***	**five** ファイブ 5 ***go***
six シックス 6 ***roku***	**seven** セブン 7 ***shichi/nana***	**eight** エイト 8 ***hachi***	**nine** ナイン 9 ***ku/kyū***	**ten** テン 10 ***jū***

twelve(o'clock) トゥエルブ(オクロック) 12 時 *jūni-ji*	

minutes ミニッツ 分 *fun/pun*	**seconds** セカンズ 秒 *byo*
five minutes ファイブ ミニッツ 5分 *go-fun*	**ten minutes** テン ミニッツ 10分 *ju-ppun*
fifteen minutes フィフティーン ミニッツ 15分 *jū-go-fun*	**half** ハーフ 半 *han*
thirty minutes サーティ ミニッツ 30分 *san-ju-ppun*	**fourty five minutes** フォーティー ファイブ ミニッツ 45分 *yon-jū-go-fun*
morning モーニング 朝 *asa*	**noon** ヌーン 昼（正午） *hiru(shōgo)*
evening イヴニング 夕方 *yūgata*	**night** ナイト 夜 *yoru*
midnight ミッドナイト 真夜中 *mayonaka*	**during the morning** デュアリング ダ モーニング 午前中 *gozen chū*

Clock labels:
- **ten** テン / 10 時 *jū-ji*
- **eleven** イレブン / 11 時 *jūichi-ji*
- **One** ワン / 1 時 *ichi-ji*
- **two** トゥー / 2 時 *ni-ji*
- **nine** ナイン / 9 時 *ku-ji*
- **three** スリー / 3 時 *san-ji*
- **eight** エイト / 8 時 *hachi-ji*
- **seven** セブン / 7 時 *shichi-ji*
- **six** シックス / 6 時 *roku-ji*
- **five** ファイブ / 5 時 *go-ji*
- **four** フォー / 4 時 *yo-ji*

afternoon アフタヌーン 午後 *gogo*	**Monday** マンデー 月曜日 *getsu-yō-bi*	**Tuesday** テューズデー 火曜日 *kayō-bi*	**Wednesday** ウェンズデー 水曜日 *suiyō-bi*
Thursday サァスデー 木曜日 *mokuyō-bi*	**Friday** フライデー 金曜日 *kinyō-bi*	**Saturday** サタデー 土曜日 *doyō-bi*	**Sunday** サンデー 日曜日 *nichiyo-bi*
January ジャニュアリー 1月 *ichi-gatsu*	**February** フェブラリー 2月 *ni-gatsu*	**March** マーチ 3月 *san-gatsu*	**April** エイプリル 4月 *shi-gatsu*
May メイ 5月 *go-gatsu*	**June** ジュン 6月 *roku-gatsu*	**July** ジュライ 7月 *shichi-gatsu*	**August** オウガスト 8月 *hachi-gatsu*
September セプテンバー 9月 *ku-gatsu*	**October** オクトーバー 10月 *jū-gatsu*	**November** ノーベンバー 11月 *jūichi-gatsu*	**December** ディッセンバー 12月 *jūni-gatsu*

today トゥデイ 今日 **kyō**	yesterday イェスタデー 昨日 **kinō**	tomorrow トゥモロー 明日 **ashita**	this week ディス　ウィーク 今週 **konshū**
next week ネクスト　ウィーク 来週 **raishū**	last week ラスト　ウィーク 先週 **senshū**	this month ディス　マンス 今月 **kongetsu**	next month ネクスト　マンス 来月 **raigetsu**
last month ラスト　マンス 先月 **sengetsu**	this year ディス　イヤー 今年 **kotoshi**	next year ネクスト　イヤー 来年 **rainen**	last year ラスト　イヤー 去年 **kyonen**
holiday ホリデー 休日 **kyūjitsu**	national holiday ナショナル　ホリデー 祝祭日 **shukusaijitsu**	weekend ウィークエンド 週末 **shūmatsu**	summer break サマーブレイク 夏休み **natsu-yasumi**
golden week ゴールデンウィーク ゴールデンウィーク **gōruden-uīku**	anniversary アニヴァーサリー 記念日 **kinenbi**	秋春 冬夏	season シーズン 季節 **kisetsu**
spring スプリング 春 **haru**	summer サマー 夏 **natsu**	autumn オータム 秋 **aki**	winter ウインター 冬 **fuyu**
weather ウェザー 天気 **tenki**	sunny サニー 晴れ **hare**	rain レイン 雨 **ame**	snow スノー 雪 **yuki**
	cloudy クラウディ くもり **kumori**	The weather is nice. ザ　ウェザー　イズ　ナイス いい天気ですね **ii tenki desune**	hot ホット 暑い **atsui**
humid ヒューミッド 蒸し暑い **mushi-atsui**	warm ウォーム 暖かい **atatakai**	cool クール 涼しい **suzushii**	cold コールド 寒い **samui**
rainy season レイニー　シーズン 梅雨 **tsuyu**	typhoon タイフーン 台風 **taifū**	earthquake アースクエイク 地震 **jishin**	tsunami ツナミ 津波 **tsunami**

104

Sightseeing
見る *Miru*

What areas in Kyoto do you recommend?
ホワット エリアズ イン キョウト ドゥ ユー リコメンド
京都のおすすめスポットはどこですか？
kyoto no osusume supotto wa dokodesuka

How long does it take to get there?
ハウ ロング ダズ イット テイク トゥ ゲット ゼア
時間はどのくらいかかりますか？
jikan wa donokurai kakari masu ka

It's very close. It's about five minutes walk.
イッツ ベリー クロス イッツ アバウト ファイヴ ミニッツ ウォーク
とても近いですよ。歩いて5分ぐらいです
totemo chikai desu yo aruite go-fun gurai desu

Please tell me the way.
プリーズ テル ミー ザ ウェイ
行き方を教えてください
iki kata o oshiete kudasai

Where are we right now?
ホェア アー ウィ ライト ナウ
ここはどこですか？
koko wa doko desu ka

Could you please write it down?
クッジュー プリーズ ライト イット ダウン
紙に書いてください
kami ni kaite kudasai

How much will it cost?
ハウ マッチ ウィル イット コスト
お金はどのくらいかかりますか？
okane wa donokurai kakari masuka

What time does it start?
ホワット タイム ダズ イット スタート
何時からですか？
nanji kara desu ka

Are we going to make it?
アー ウィー ゴーイング トゥ メイク イット
間に合いますか？
maniai masu ka

Will you take a picture of us?
ウィル ユー テイク ア ピクチャー オブ アス
写真を撮ってください
shashin o totte kudasai

Please take your shoes off.
プリーズ テイク ユア シューズ オフ
靴を脱いでください
kutsu o nuide kudasai

I'm looking for a rest room.
アイム ルッキング フォー ア レスト ルーム
トイレを探しています
toire o sagashite imasu

I have never seen anything like this before.
アイ ハヴ ネヴァー シーン エニシング ライク ディス ビフォア
こんなもの初めて見ました
kon na mono hajimete mimashita

I like it here. アイ ライク イット ヒア ここが好きです *kokoga suki desu*	**unbelievable** アンビリーバブル 信じられない *shinjirarenai*	**very rare** ヴェリー レア とても珍しい *totemo mezurashī*

wonderful ワンダフル すばらしい *subarashī*	**great** グレイト すごい *sugoi*	**not a big deal** ノット ア ビッグ ディール たいしたことない *taishitakotonai*	**interesting** インタレスティング おもしろい *omoshiroi*
beautiful ビューティフル きれい *kirei*	**dirty** ダーティー 汚い *kitanai*	**not so good** ノット ソー グッド いまいち *imaichi*	**quite** クワイト かなり *kanari*
this way ディス ウェイ こっち *kotchi*	**that way** ダット ウェイ あっち *atchi*	**over there** オーヴァー デア そっち *sotchi*	**straight** ストレート まっすぐ *massugu*
near ニア 近い *chikai*	**far** ファー 遠い *tōi*	**right(left)side** ライト（レフト）サイド 右（左）側 *migi(hidari)gawa*	**turn right(left)** ターン ライト（レフト） 右（左）へ曲がる *migi(hidari) e magaru*

Meals
食べる *Taberu*

I am hungry.
アイ アム ハングリー

おなかがすきました
onaka ga sukimashita

What do you want to eat?
ホァット ドゥ ユー ウォント トゥ イート

何が食べたい?
nani ga tabetai

How much do you want to spend?
ハウ マッチ ドゥ ユー ウォント トゥ スペンド

予算はどれくらいですか?
yosan wa dorekuraidesu ka

I'd like to reserve a table.
アイド ライク トゥ リザーブ ア テーブル

予約をお願いします
yoyaku o onegaishimasu

I (don't)have a reservation.
アイ (ドント) ハブ ア リザベーション

予約しています (していません)
yoyaku shiteimasu/shiteimasen

May I have a menu?
メアイ ハヴ ア メニュー

メニューを下さい
menyū o kudasai

What do you recommend?
ホァット ドゥ ユー レコメンド?

おすすめは何ですか?
osusume wa nan desu ka

Please give me a large serving.
プリーズ ギヴ ミー ア ラージ サービング

大盛りでお願いします
ōmori de onegai shimasu

I can't eat this.
アイ キャント イート ディス

これは食べられません
kore wa taberaremasen

I'm allergic to peanuts.
アイ アム アレルジック トゥ ピーナッツ

ピーナッツアレルギーがあります
pīnattsu arerugī ga arimasu

Could you tell me how to eat this?
クッジュー テル ミー ハウ トゥ イート ディス

食べ方を教えてください
tabekata o oshiete kudasai

Another bowl, please!
アナザー ボウル プリーズ

おかわりを下さい!
okawari o kudasai

Cheers!
チアーズ!

乾杯!
kanpai

I'm thirsty.
アイム タースティ

のどが渇きました
nodoga kawakimashita

A cup of hot tea, please.
ア カップ オブ ホット ティー プリーズ

あたたかいお茶をください
atatakai ocha o kudasai

I'm full.
アイム フル

おなかがいっぱいです
onaka ga ippai desu

Thank you for the meal.
サンキュー フォー ダ ミール

ごちそうさま
gochisō-sama

It's on me.
イッツ オン ミー

私のおごりです
watashi no ogori desu

Let's split the bill.
レッツ スプツット ダ ビル

割り勘にしましょう
warikan ni shimashō

Can I have the bill?
キャン アイ ハヴ ダ ビル?

お勘定お願いします
okanjō onegai shimasu

Can I use my card?
キャン アイ ユーズ マイ カード

カードは使えますか?
kādo wa tsukae masu ka

Is service included in the bill?
イズ サービス インクルーディッド イン ダ ビル

サービス料込ですか?
sābisu ryō komi desu ka

May I smoke?
メイ アイ スモーク

タバコを吸ってもいいですか?
tabako o sutte mo iidesu ka

Japanese food ジャパニーズ　フード 日本料理 ***nihon-ryōri***	Chinese food チャイニーズ　フード 中国料理 ***chūgoku-ryōri***	Korean food コリアン　フード 韓国料理 ***kankoku-ryōri***	French food フレンチ　フード フランス料理 ***furansu-ryōri***
breakfast ブレックファスト 朝食 ***chōshoku***	lunch ランチ 昼食 ***chūshoku***	dinner ディナー 夕食 ***yūshoku***	snack スナック おやつ ***oyatsu***
beef ビーフ 牛肉 ***gyūniku***	pork ポーク 豚肉 ***butaniku***	chicken チキン 鶏肉 ***toriniku***	fish フィッシュ 魚 ***sakana***
beer ビア ビール ***bīru***	hot sake ホット　サケ 熱燗 ***atsukan***	cold sake コールド　サケ 冷 ***hiya***	hangover ハングオーバー 二日酔い ***futsukayoi***
		clear liquor クリア　リカー 焼酎 ***shōchū***	specialty food スペシャリティ　フード 名物料理 ***meibutsu-ryōri***
milk ミルク 牛乳 ***gyūnyū*** MILK	vegetables ヴェジタブルズ 野菜 ***yasai***	fruit フルートゥ 果物 ***kudamono***	rice balls ライス　ボールズ おにぎり ***onigiri***
miso soup ミソ　スープ みそしる ***misoshiru***	lunch box ランチ　ボックス お弁当 ***obentō***	toothpicks トゥースピックス つまようじ ***tsumayōji***	wet towel ウェット　タオル おしぼり ***oshibori***
This is very good. ディス　イズ　ヴェリー　グッド 超おいしいです ***chō oishī desu***	delicious デリシャス おいしいですね ***oishī desune***	so-so ソウ　ソウ まあまあ ***māmā***	This is awful. ディス　イズ　オーフル まずい ***mazui***

bitter ビター 苦い ***nigai***	salty ソルティ しょっぱい ***shoppai***	sour サワー すっぱい ***suppai***	sweet スイート 甘い ***amai***	hot ホット 辛い ***karai***

taste strong/thick
テイスト　ストロング／ティック
味が濃い（薄い）
aji ga koi (usui)

107

Shopping
買う **Kau**

cash キャッシュ 現金 *genkin*	consumption tax コンサンプション　タックス 消費税 *shōhizei*

How much is this? ハウ　マッチ　イズ　ディス これはいくらですか？ *korewa ikura desu ka*	Please give me a discount. プリーズ　ギヴ　ミー　ア　ディスカウント まけてください *makete kudasai*	Your change is fifty yen. ユアー　チェンジ　イズ　フィフティー　エン おつりは 50 円です *otsuri wa gojū en desu*	Please exchange. プリーズ　イクスチェンジ 両替してください *ryōgae shitekudasai*
Do you have a cheaper (more expensive) one? ドゥ　ユー　ハヴ　ア　チーパー　（モア　エクスペンシヴ）ワン もっと安い（高い）ものはありますか？ *motto yasui(takai)mono wa arimasu ka*		Too expensive トゥ　エクスペンシヴ 高すぎます *takasugimasu*	I want to buy this. アイ　ウォント　トゥ　バイ　ディス これを買いたいです。 *kore o kaitai desu*
Do you have a bigger (smaller) one? ドゥ　ユー　ハヴ　ア　ビッガー　（スモーラー）ワン もっと大きい（小さい）ものはありますか？ *motto ōkii(chii-sai)mono wa arimasu ka*		Do you have this in other sizes? ドゥ　ユー　ハヴ　ディス　イン　アザー　サイズィーズ 他のサイズはありますか？ *hoka no saizu wa arimasu ka*	
Can I try it on? キャン　アイ　トライ　イット　オン 試着していいですか？ *shichaku shite īdesu ka*	Which one is popular? フィッチ　ワン　イズ　ポピュラー どれが人気ですか？ *dorega ninki desu ka*	What colors do you have? ホアット　カラーズ　ドゥ　ユー　ハヴ 何色がありますか？ *nani-iro ga arimasu ka*	
I'm just looking. アイム　ジャスト　ルッキング 見ているだけです *miteiru dake desu*	May I see it? メイ　アイ　シー　イット 見せてください *misete kudasai*	This is popular. ディス　イズ　ポピュラー これは流行っています *kore wa hayatte imasu*	I can't decide which one. アイ　キャント　デサイド　フィッチ　ワン 迷っています *mayotteimasu*
This is fragile. ディス　イズ　フラジール これは壊れものです *kore wa kowaremono desu*	I would like to send this. アイ　ウッド　ライク　トゥ　センド　ディス これを送りたいです *kore o okuritai desu*	Please wrap it nicely. プリーズ　ラップ　イット　ナイスリー キレイに包んでください *kirei ni tsutsunde kudasai*	souvenir スーヴェニア おみやげ *omiyage*
looks good ルックス　グッド 似合う *niau*	cute キュート かわいい *kawaii*	cosmetics コスメティックス コスメ *kosume*	accessories アクセサリーズ アクセサリー *akusesari*

one yen coin ワン　エン　コイン 1円玉 *ichi en dama*	five yen coin ファイブ　エン　コイン 5円玉 *go en dama*	ten yen coin テン　エン　コイン 10 円玉 *jū en dama*	fifty yen coin フィフティー　エン　コイン 50 円玉 *go-jū en dama*	a hundred yen coin ア　ハンドレッド　エン　コイン 100 円玉 *hyaku en dama*	five hundred yen coin ファイブ　ハンドレッド　エン　コイン 500 円玉 *go-hyaku en dama*

a thousand yen bill ア　サウザンド　エン　ビル 千円札 *sen en satsu*	two thousand yen bill トゥー　サウザンド　エン　ビル 二千円札 *ni-sen en satsu*	five thousand yen bill ファイブ　サウザンド　エン　ビル 五千円札 *go-sen en satsu*	ten thousand yen bill テン　サウザンド　エン　ビル 一万円札 *ichi-man en satsu*

Trouble
トラブル *Toraburu*

Help me! ヘルプ ミー 助けて! ***tasukete***	**Stop it!** ストップ イット やめてください ***yamete kudasai***

groper グローパー 痴漢 ***chikan***	**thief** ティーフ 泥棒 ***dorobō***	**medicine** メディスィン 薬 ***kusuri***	**doctor** ドクター 医者 ***isha***

What's wrong? ホアッツ ウロング どうしましたか? ***dō shimashita ka***	**I'm lost.** アイム ロスト 道に迷いました ***michi ni mayoimashita***

I'm OK. アイム オーケー 大丈夫です ***daijoubu desu***	**My wallet was stolen.** マイ ウォレット ワズ ストールン 財布を取られました ***saifu o toraremashita***

finger フィンガー 指 *yubi*

hand ハンド 手 *te*

eyebrow アイブロー 眉 *mayu*

forehead フォアヘッド 額 *hitai*

head ヘッド 頭 *atama*

ear イアー 耳 *mimi*

nose ノウズ 鼻 *hana*

eye アイ 目 *me*

jaw ジョー あご *ago*

tongue タング 舌 *shita*

shoulder ショルダー 肩 *kata*

throat スロート のど *nodo*

chest チェスト 胸 *mune*

back バック 背中 *senaka*

midriff ミドリフ みぞおち *mizo-ochi*

abdomen アブドメン 腹 *hara*

arm アーム 腕 *ude*

navel ネイブル へそ *heso*

elbow エルボー ひじ *hiji*

knee ニー ひざ *hiza*

nail ネイル ツメ *tsume*

wrist リスト 手首 *tekubi*

skin スキン 肌 *hada*

leg レッグ 足 *ashi*

toe トゥ つま先 *tsumasaki*

ankle アンクル 足首 *ashikubi*

calf カウフ ふくらはぎ *fukurahagi*

I have a headache. アイ ハヴァ ヘディック 頭が痛い ***atama ga itai***

I don't feel good. アイ ドント フィール グッド 具合が悪い ***guai ga warui***

I was injured. アイ ワズ インジュアド 怪我をしました ***kega o shimashita***

I have a fever. アイ ハヴァ フィーヴァー 熱があります ***netsu ga arimasu***

Where is the nearest hospital (police box)? ウェア イズ ニアレスト ホスピタル (ポリスボックス) この近くの病院 (交番) はどこですか? ***kono chikaku no byouin(kōban)wa doko desu ka?***

My blood type is A. マイ ブラッド タイプ イズ エイ 私の血液型は A 型です ***watashi no ketsueki gata wa ē gata desu***

INDEX 索引